TOPOSAURUS

TOPOSAURUS

A Humorous Treasury of Top • o • nyms*

John D. Jacobson

The Word Sleuth

*An entertaining assortment of familiar words and phrases derived from place names—and their colorful origins

John Wiley & Sons, Inc.

NEW YORK • CHICHESTER • BRISBANE • TORONTO • SINGAPORE

Recognizing the importance of preserving what has been written, it is a policy of John Wiley & Sons, Inc. to have books of enduring value published in the United States printed on acid-free paper, and we exert our best efforts to that end.

Publisher: Therese Zak
Editor: Steve Ross
Managing Editor: Kate Bradford
Editing, Design, Production: Laura Cleveland, WordCrafters Editorial Services, Inc.

Published by John Wiley & Sons, Inc.

Library of Congress Cataloging-in-Publication Data

Jacobson, John D.
Toposaurus : a humorous treasury of toponyms / John D. Jacobson.
p. cm.
Includes bibliographical references.
ISBN 0-471-52772-6
1. English language—Etymology—Dictionaries. 2. English language—Foreign words and phrases—Dictionaries. 3. Names. Geographical. 4. Toponymy. I. Title.
PE1582.A3J3 1990
422'.03—dc20

90-34329
CIP

Printed in the United States of America

90 91 10 9 8 7 6 5 4 3 2 1

To Josephine—wife, friend, and confidante—who has aided and supported me on this project and throughout my adult life.

Preface

A very wise man once said, "One should never watch sausages or laws being made." Watching new words develop, however, or learning how current words were originally coined is another matter.

I have been fascinated with *etymology* (the study of word and phrase origins) as far back as I can remember and have been seriously tracing words for years. When I first started tracking the origins of words, I began to assign each word, where possible, to a specific category. One category that has special interest for me is *toponyms*, or words that come from place names. The word *toponym* combines two Greek elements, *topos* meaning place and *onoma* meaning name, or words that are derived from place names. Toponyms are especially fascinating to me because they reach deep into the spheres of geography and world history, as well as etymology. These essays, then, provide an absorbing way to learn about world and word histories.

It takes a great deal of presumption, especially for an etymologist, to coin a new word (*neologism*), since there are already so many English words (lexicographers William and Mary Morris estimate that there are three to five million words in the English language if one includes slang, cant, and scientific words). Thousands of new words are created each year, but only a small percentage of these ever attain the status of standard English usage. One special characteristic of the English language, and one of the reasons it has become one of the most widely spoken of the world's nearly three thousand official languages, is its infinite capacity to accommodate novel ideas, fashions, products, scientific breakthroughs, and political and social changes with new words. The daily rain of neologisms in both spoken and written English contribute to the unending river of words that are either filtered out or accepted by the vast jury of English speakers who ultimately determine what new words reach lexicographical (dictionary) stardom. In considering a title or description for this book, I coined the neologism, *toposaurus,* to best describe what this book is all about. Toposaurus combines the Greek elements *topos* and *saurus. Saurus,* the last element in *thesaurus,* means "treasure." So, this neologism, *toposaurus,* quite literally fits the definition of its elements and can be defined as "a treasury of words and phrases derived from place names, and the etymology thereof."

Toponyms are not always recognizable as such. For example, who would expect the word *hooker,* meaning "prostitute," to come from the name of an old section of New York City where women of the night once plied their trade? Or, who would guess that a *sleazy* group of words, including *sleazy, sleazo, sleazemonger* and *sleazebucket* were derived from a once very fine fabric originally made in Silesia, now a part of Poland? The fabric family, except for synthetic fabrics, is predominantly toponymic and I have, therefore, woven quite a few samples into this text, including *calico, cashmere, chantilly lace, cambric,* and *jersey.* I have also incorporated the *jeaneology* (sic) of three fabrics that have become synonymous with a very popular item of apparel, namely, *denims, jeans,* and *dungarees.*

In addition to fabric, I have included a number of interesting categories (despite the fact that the words contained herein are not arranged by classification, but alphabetically). Here are a few of the major categories and some examples of their featured words:

Food baloney, hamburger, frankfurter, cajun, cantaloupe, melba toast, and mayonnaise.

Dance Charleston, flamenco, malaguena, tarantella.

Ethnic slurs honky, gringo, chicano, bohunk.

Color canary yellow, chartreuse, Coventry blue, indigo, magenta.

Clothing bikini, cravat, derby, tuxedo, ascot, galosh.

Human behavior stoicism, lush, barbarian, welsher, cannibal, frank, laconic, spartan, lesbian, lethargy, sardonic.

Vehicles coach, limousine, landau.

Special commodities cologne, venetian blinds, copper, turquoise, tobacco.

Biblical Bible, bible, good samaritan.

Oddities ghetto, vaudeville, mall, OK, utopia, pompadour, spa, Spanish Fly, serendipity.

Quite a few toponyms have been excluded from this book. The test for a word's inclusion was that it met several of the following criteria:

1. It should have an interesting historical content (Armageddon, Canossa, Cannae). Such words may seem obscure, but the stories of their origins are truly fascinating.
2. It should not readily be perceived as being derived from a placename, for example, OK, gyp, suede, academy, lumber, limo, bible, and copper.
3. In all cases, the word must be included in a current major dictionary.
4. I have, wherever possible, selected toponyms that have some meaning other than simply the designation of a

> place. For instance, while Hackney, England, is easily recognized as a borough of London, it is also a designation for a breed of horse from Hackney. Its equine connection has resulted in several diverse meanings, including an ordinary or uncreative writer, as well as the four-wheeled modern taxi.

I generally have excluded words used to describe wines, animal breeds, and the like that can be easily found classified in any encyclopedia. I also have avoided obvious toponyms and those that offer no special intellectual rewards.

This toposaurus was designed for people who love words, and that includes most of the seven hundred million English speakers of the world. It was not created for the practicing or professional etymologist, although such a person should especially enjoy it. Each essay was written to stimulate, to provide a historical perspective, and to amuse. Each etymology was meticulously researched and is, for the most part, devoid of personal speculation. The subjects are arranged alphabetically for easy location, and cross-references to other words described in the book are noted in boldface type. I hope you enjoy the fruit of my efforts as much as I delighted in bringing it to you. Perhaps this little book will inspire you to become, like myself, a serious, albeit amateur student of etymology. If so, I have included an extensive bibliography of books, most of which are still in print, for those who wish to pursue etymology more seriously.

TOPOSAURUS

academy/academic

How did the name of a brave warrior become associated with places of higher learning? The story is certainly not *academic,* even though the word is. This word origin begins with the story of Akademos, an ancient Greek hero of the Trojan War. The Greeks were so pleased with Akademos' heroism that they established a garden grove in his honor near Athens. Years later, Plato, the third-century B.C. philosopher, established a school in that grove.

By the fifteenth century, *Akademos* had passed into English as *academy,* Plato's school. A century later, the Plato connection was forgotten and *academy* came to mean a place of higher learning. The meaning of *academic* currently ranges from scholarly to theoretical and without practical purpose.

Acapulco gold. See **marijuana.**

Aceldama

In the New Testament, Judas was the apostle who betrayed Jesus to the priests and elders for 30 pieces of silver. Judas' family name, Iscariot, probably came from the Latin word *sicarius* meaning murderer. Judas belonged to an anti-Roman terrorist group called the Sacarii. The Sacarii were similar to the Zealots of which another apostle, Simon Zealotes, was a member. It was the Zealots (from the Greek word *zelos*, meaning zeal) who defended themselves from the Romans at Masada from A.D. 66 to 73.

In Acts i, 18 it is said that Judas "bought a field with the reward of his wickedness." The field so purchased was known as *Aceldama*, a word that came from the Aramaic language and means field of carnage, slaughter, or butchery. It was here that Judas is said to have thrown himself down upon the rocks and killed himself. *Aceldama* was used as a burial place for foreigners. Today, despite Judas' duplicity, *Aceldama* is used as a metaphor for bloodshed or slaughter because of its ancient and original Aramaic meaning.

Aeolian/aeolian/ aeolian harp or lyre

Aeolis was an ancient country of northwest Asia Minor including the island of Lesbos (see **lesbian**). Aeolus (with a "u") was the reputed founder of these people, as well as the god of the winds ruling the Aeolian Islands. In the *Odyssey*, presumably written by Homer, Aeolus gave Odysseus "the contrary winds tied up in a bag," but sailors let them out and their ship was blown off course. Aeolus also blew several words and phrases our way, one of which may be music to your ears.

Aeolian one of four main divisions of the prehistoric Greeks (Achean, **Dorian**, Ionian, and Aeolian).

aeolian lower-cased when referring to the winds.

aeolian harp or lyre a box with an opening across which are stretched a number of strings of equal length; the strings are sounded by the wind.

afghan

Fabrics are often named after the places where they were first woven. The *afghan,* an excellent example of a fabric toponym, is a soft woolen blanket or shawl usually crocheted or knitted. It is designed with a series of geometric patterns of varying size and with vivid colorings.

The *afghan* is, of course, a product of Afghanistan, a republic in south Asia. It is northwest of India, east of Iran, and south of the Soviet Union. At one time, Afghanistan was a part of the Persian and Alexandrian Empires. The Soviet Union recently tried to annex it as well, but was unable to persuade the fiercely independent Afghans to go along with its plans. The word *afghan,* used as a name for the region's uniquely designed blankets, first appeared in print in 1833. However, I have found no explanation for how the name *afghan* came to be applied to similar blankets and shawls knitted today the world over.

As long as we're barking up this tree, it's worth noting that an *Afghan* hound is the name of a very large slender dog originally bred in Afghanistan.

Afrikaner/Afro-/Afro-Saxon/ African golf

The noted etymologist Eric Partridge suggests that the Latin word *Africa* and its Greek counterpart *Aphrike* were both derived from a Phoenician name for the land of Carthage; this name was eventually extended to the entire continent. There are several toponyms derived from this continent where the Phoenicians once built the great city of Carthage on its northern coast.

On the southern tip of Africa are the *Afrikaner,* white, native-born South Africans of either Dutch or Huguenot origin. The *Afrikaners,* or Boers, fought the English for control of South Africa in two contests known as the Boer Wars. For the most part, the word *African* is reserved for black people who were born in or who migrated from Africa. *Afro-* was originally a combining form indicating African descent (i.e., Afro-American), but in the 1970s it was popularly used to describe the Afro-American hairstyle in which the hair is allowed to grow naturally. An *Afro-Saxon,* according to Robert Chapman's *American Slang,* is a satirical term for a black person who has assumed the behavior and values of the dominant white society.

Our final African derivative is *African golf,* a slang term for craps, so called because of its racist and patently false assumption that craps was a weakness primarily of Afro-American people.

agate

According to Pliny the Elder, *agate,* a semiprecious stone of quartz marked with bands of color, was originally named *achate* after the Achates River in Sicily where these stones were first found.

Agates are made of chalcedony, but to generations of young people, an agate was an extremely hard spheroid with which one played marbles (mibs). If you played poorly you could *lose all your agates (marbles),* an expression that has come to mean to become silly, irrational, or senile. The Elder Pliny, apparently, never lost his marbles. In fact, there are those who believe that it was this Pliny who discovered the first "hard rock" group which he called the "Agates."

alabaster

In the lyrics of the song, *America the Beautiful*, the author, Katherine Lee Bates (1859–1929), uses *alabaster* as an adjective: "Thine *alabaster* cities gleam undimmed by human tears." Perhaps American cities do have that soft *alabaster* look in a certain light, but you would have to travel to England, France, or Italy to find large deposits of this marblelike material. *Alabaster* is a soft, fine, translucent variety of gypsum, occurring in white, yellow, and red. Occasionally, it is mottled like marble. *Alabaster* is most often used to create lamp bases, vessels, and statues.

Most authorities attribute the origin of this word to a town in upper (southern) Egypt, Alabastron, where deposits of this stone were found in ancient times. There are other sources, however, that hold to the theory that *alabaster* is derived from the Egyptian *a la baste,* literally "vessel of (the goddess) Bast."

Albion. See **English.**

allemande/allemande sauce

"Grab your partner
and do - si - do
With your partner allemande
Now give yourself
a great big hand."

While this square-dance "call" might be met with confused or angry stares from square-dance afficionados, I risked their opprobrium in order to introduce one of a number of toponymous dance steps (see also **polka, malaguena,** and **tarantella**), the *allemande.* The *allemande right and left* elements used in modern square-dancing can be traced back to a dance of the seventeenth century.

One noted authority concludes that it is derived from the French dance that was called *l'Allemande,* the German Woman, while another expert suggests that it came from *dance allemande,* German dance. Both versions can be traced to the Latin word for Germany, *Allemania. Allemande sauce,* a sauce that is thickened and enriched with egg yolks, is actually a French sauce inspired by the Germans.

Altaic/Ural-Altaic

In A.D. 896, a wild barbarian tribe of horsemen known as Magyars swept into the broad plain of the Danube River in what is present-day Hungary. The Magyars came from the region of the *Ural-Altaic* mountains that stretch from Russia through Outer Mongolia and China to the Pacific. *Altaic* means gold in the Mongolian language. Today, the Altaic people include the Turks, Mongols, and Manchiu-Tungus. In 1730, F.J. Van Stralenberg proposed the use of *Altaic* to describe this language group whose speakers stretch from Europe to the Pacific. He also proposed *using Altaic to refer to* the larger *Ural-Altaic* group of languages that includes Finnic, Hungarian, and Samoyedic (spoken in Siberia) which is also known as the Finno-Ugric group. The Finnish and Hungarian languages, in addition to Basque, are the only languages in Europe that are not a part of the Indo-European family, which includes Italian, Slavic, Baltic, Hellenic, Celtic, German, English, Spanish, Latin, Greek, Russian, Albanian, Lithuanian, Armenian, Persian, Hindi, and Hittite.

The *Ural-Altaic* invaders of Hungary eventually were converted to Christianity in the late tenth century, but the language of the Magyars remains the official language of that country to this day. A German, Johann Blumenback (1752—1840), used the name of a mountain group, the Caucasus to refer to a racial type (see **caucasian**). It is appropriate that another German, Van

Stralenberg, also went to the mountain top to label a language group, the *Altaic* and *Ural-Altaic*.

amen. See **ammonia.**

America's Cup

How did the quadrennial *America's Cup* international yachting event, which originated in England, get its Yankee name? Tack along with me as I reveal the answer to this question and provide some interesting related trivia as well.

This story begins in 1851 when an American entry won a 53-mile sailboat race around the English Isle of Wight. The race, which at that time was known as the "100 Guinea Cup," was won by the crew of the upstart U.S. boat, *America*. In 1857, the syndicate that built the *America* presented a cup to the New York Yacht Club. This cup became a perpetual trophy and was much sought after by competing yachts the world over.

The trophy, which thereafter became known as the *America's Cup*, has been dominated by the American sailing fraternity ever since. In 1983, the cup left our shores when an Australian entry won the race. But in early 1987, Dennis Connor triumphantly brought the cup back to U.S. shores.

amino. See **ammonia.**

ammonia/amino/ammonite/ amen

This etymology may seem like so much camel droppings, because according to noted etymologist Eric Partridge, that is actually the source of the word *ammonia*. Our search for this origin takes us to the oasis of Siwa in the Libyan desert at the site of the ruins of an ancient temple dedicated to the Egyptian god, Amon-Re, The Hidden One. The Greeks adopted this god and called him Zeus, which the Romans converted to Jupiter (a combination of Zeus-Pater, The Father of the Heavens). Alexander the Great is known to have consulted the oracle at the Amon-Re Temple at Siwa, as did many lesser mortals over the millennia. According to Eric Partridge, the *sal ammoniac* (salt of ammoniac) found near the temple was the result of the enormous buildup of camel dung and urine deposited there over many centuries.

Amon-Re was often depicted wearing ram's horns, which Alexander is said to have adopted as a decoration for his helmet. Amon-Re's power was so great that his name was often incorporated into the names of Egyptian rulers, such as Tut-Ankh-Amun. Other English words inspired by the ram's horn symbol of Amon-Re include *amino,* a kind of acid, and *ammonite,* a ram-shaped fossil. Today, *ammonia* is found in humus-rich soils, sea water, and plants, as well as in animal wastes such as camel droppings.

Much later, the Hebrews adopted the name of this Egyptian, *Amon,* gave it a new spelling, *amen,* and a new meaning, so be it. The Hebrews passed it on to the Greeks and it survives today as an ending to prayers, creeds, and, sometimes, discussions about *ammonia, amino, ammonite,* and *amen.*

ammonite. See **ammonia.**

Anglican. See **English.**

Angora/angora

Ankara is the name of a province in west central Turkey. It is also the name of Turkey's capital city, which has a population of over two million. Prior to 1930, Ankara was known as *Angora*. For thousands of years this region was known for the special *Angora* goats and rabbits raised there.

The *Angora* goat has long hair which is known as *mohair*. While the size of the mohair fiber is comparable to wool, the former has a much smoother handle than wool. Mohair is derived from the Arab word *muhkayyar*, a fabric, and is often combined with other fibers to produce a blend used in men's summer suits. From *mohair*, the French fashioned the word *moiré*, a mohair fabric with a watered pattern.

The *Angora* rabbit hair is also used as a textile and, because of its softness, it is often used in making women's sweaters. The hair of the rabbit is plucked while the goat's is shorn. The *Angora* cat is also indigenous to *Angora*, but to the best of my knowledge, its hair is not used for textiles. You will note that *Angora* becomes lower-cased when referring to a garment such as an *angora* sweater.

Angostura®

This is the sweet success story of bitters—*Angostura* aromatic bitters. *Angostura* bitters was the brainchild of its founder, Dr. J.G.B. Siegert, a surgeon in Simon Bolivar's army of liberation in Venezuela in the 1820s. Siegert was searching for a medicine that would cure the stomach ailments suffered by Bolivar's soldiers. He first introduced his patent medicine in 1824, but it was not until 1850, after years of experimentation, that he started to export his elixir.

Angostura was the name of the town where Siegert first produced his bitters. The name of that town was later changed to Ciudad Bolivar. In the 1870s, the Siegert family moved their manufacturing facilities to Trinidad where they continued to produce bitters, as well as rum, to this day. Today, according to its makers, *Angostura* aromatic bitters is promoted throughout the world as a "stimulant to the appetite, a stomatica, and to ease flatulence." Because of its unique aroma and flavor, it is also a popular ingredient in alcoholic beverages and in cooking.

antimacassar. See **macassar.**

Appaloosa

The *Appaloosa* is one of a hardy breed of western riding horses that was bred by the Nez Perce Indians of Idaho. It is easily distinguished by the remarkable mottled markings on its hide. The breed was probably named for the Palouse River which the French called *a la Palouse.*

There is speculation that the slang word *lollapalooza,* which means something outstanding of its kind, was inspired by the unusual looking *Appaloosa*—very definitely a *lollapaloosa* as horses go.

apple/apple of one's eye/ applesauce/apple-pie order

The *apple* is one of a number of fruits whose names are derived from places. The tangerine, for example, is derived from Tangiers, a city in northern Morocco, while the source of the peach is the Greek word *Persikos,* meaning things pertaining to Persia, an ancient empire known today as Iran. At the core of this toponym is the Latin term for *apple, nux avellina,* a nut of Abella, a region of Campania, Italy, that was rich in apples. I shall further nourish your etymological curiosity by peeling away the mystery of several appetizing idioms.

apple of one's eye According to William and Mary Morris and Wilfred Funk, the *pupil* in Anglo-Saxon times meant both eye and *apple.* The pupil was considered very precious. Accordingly, a child, grandchild, or any other special person might be referred to as simply precious, or the *apple of one's eye*.

applesauce a comestible that has come to mean nonsense, a sense that has been traced particularly to the boarding-house custom of serving plenty of cheap *applesauce* in lieu of the more expensive foods.

apple-pie order There is really nothing orderly about an apple pie, and in fact, this idiom originally had nothing whatsoever to do with apples. It has come to mean prim and proper, and was derived from the French expression *nappe-pli*, meaning folded linen, which you must agree usually looks pretty neat.

Arabic and Roman numerals

While it generally is presumed that *Roman numerals* preceded *Arabic numerals*, they were, in fact, developed independently at about the same time during the third century B.C. The first appearance of *Roman numerals* was on the Columna Rostrata, a monument erected in Rome to celebrate a major victory over the Carthaginians in 260 B.C. The Roman numeration was widely used in Europe up until the 1500s, when it was replaced by the more efficient Arabic variety.

Although the Arabs are generally credited with developing the *Arabic numerals*, it was actually the Hindi of India who first used the first nine numbers (1–9) in the third century B.C. The concept of zero was introduced, also by the Hindus, in the ninth century A.D. The Arabs adopted the Hindi system, also in the ninth century, and they brought it to Spain about A.D. 900, where it was quickly adopted by scholars and traders. In the fifteenth century, the printing press caused the standardization and rapid spread of the Arabic system throughout Europe.

The Arabic symbols are clearly of Hindi origin, while the Roman symbols are believed to be derived from Greek letters. The widely accepted Theodor Mommsen theory holds that the V (5) is a sort of hieroglyph representing the open hand and five fingers. The X (10) is composed of a V on top connected to an inverted V on the bottom. The C (100) is an abbreviation of the Latin word *centum,* meaning one hundred. Roman numerals are still used on clock and watch faces (where the four is usually represented as IIII instead of IV), in outlines, for dates on monuments and public buildings, for movie sequals, and in books.

arcadian

In the central Peloponnesus peninsula of Greece rests the ancient pastoral region of Arcadia. The name of this beautiful rural area has become synonymous with rustic and peaceful rural life and has been used by English authors and poets.

Arcadians should not be confused with the Acadians who were early settlers of Acadia (Nova Scotia). In anticipation of a war with the French, in 1755 the British resettled ten thousand Acadians to the lower American colonies. Some of these Acadians settled in Louisiana, and their name was corrupted to **Cajun.**

Arkansas toothpick

Arkansawyers (a variant of Arkansan) have a tendency to indulge in the use of jocular metaphors that either create a Bunyanesque view of Arkansas life or ridicule the one-time relatively primitive nature of life in that state. The *Arkansas toothpick,* which is a good example of the Bunyanesque form of this figure of speech, is a bowie knife. This metaphor has the effect of magnifying the special grand nature of Arkansas by deprecating a very large bayonet-size blade said to have been invented by

Jim Bowie (1796–1836), a Texas revolutionary leader. Here are some additional Arkansanesque idioms obtained from *DARE* (*Dictionary of American Regional English*):

Arkansas lizard a louse.

Arkansas asphalt logs laid side by side to form a corduroy road.

Arkansas fire extinguisher a chamber pot.

Arkansas dew a sudden heavy rain.

Arkansas T-bone steak bacon.

Arkansas wedding cake corn bread.

You might want to invent your own Arkansas metaphors using your *Arkansas word processor,* commonly known as a pencil.

Armageddon

According to a Biblical prophesy (Revelation 16:16), *Armageddon* will be the scene of a final battle between the forces of good and evil at the end of the world.

Armageddon is derived from the Hebrew words *Har Megiddo* which means Hill of Megiddo. Megiddo is also an ancient city of northern Palestine on the southern side of the plain of Esdraelon and the valley of Kishon, 20 miles north of Samaria. Recent excavations revealed that this town was settled in 3500 B.C. Many battles have been fought there, including Thutmose III's victory over the Syrians in 1479 B.C. and British General Allenby's victory over the Turks in 1918.

Armageddon has also come to symbolize a decisive conflict, and was popularized by Teddy Roosevelt in 1912 at the Bull Moose Party's convention in Chicago, when he shouted, "We stand at *Armageddon,* and we battle for the Lord."

artesian well

A major discovery was made in a well in the Artois province of northern France in A.D. 1100. The *artesian well,* named after its place of discovery, was first encountered there. *Artesian wells* are those in which the water rises above the surface of the ground. According to the *World Book Encyclopedia,* "artesian wells are found where an aquifer (water bearing layer of earth), that is surrounded by dense clay or rock, slopes downward. The water is trapped because it cannot pass through the clay or rock. Gravity creates pressure through the dense layer above the aquifer, and this in turn forces the water up into the drilled opening." *Artesian wells* have been known to shoot water two hundred feet up into the air when first released.

Aryan

You might be surprised to learn that the great English playwright George Bernard Shaw (1856–1950) coined the word *superman.* He used *superman* as an English translation of *ubermensch,* a word first used by Nietsche (1844–1900), a German philosopher. In 1903, Shaw even wrote a play entitled *Man and Superman.* Hitler's propaganda minister, Joseph Goebbels (1897–1945), used *superman* (*ubermensch*) as a synonym for *Aryan,* a word that he used to describe an ethnically superior person. He was convinced, and tried to convince the German people and the rest of the world, that the Nordic people were *Aryan* supermen.

Aryan was first popularized by Max Muller (1823–1900), an Anglo-German philologist. He used it as a term to describe the

Indo-European family of languages of which English and most other European languages are members. *Aryan* is derived from the Sanskrit word *arya* meaning noble. It is closely related to the Old Persian word *Arya* which was the Persian name for the eastern part of Persia. It is from this *Arya* root that modern day Iran gets its name.

Aryan has fallen into disuse as an ethnic term and as a term for our language family, the Indo-European group. It was Joseph Goebbels' use of the word during the Nazi regime of the 1930s and 1940s that made the word *Aryan* repugnant to most of the world. It is ironic that the country of Iran, which derives its name from the same source as *aryan*, is today considered repugnant to some westerners because of its inordinate hatred of the West and its policy of political terrorism.

ascot

Through the years, horse racing has inspired several new fashion styles. The English **derby,** for instance, inspired the use of the *derby* hat (also known as the *bowler*). Another famous horse race at Ascot Heath in Berkshire Heath, England, inspired several other clothing fashions including the *ascot* tie. The race was established in 1711 by Queen Anne, according to tradition.

But it was not until the 1890s that a loose-fitting tie or scarf, fastened with a stickpin, was named after the famous track. The tie, along with *ascot* hats and dresses, was worn in the Royal Enclosure at the racecourse. Only the necktie, which has now lost much of its original popularity, remains in use today (to the best of my knowledge) and retains the *ascot* name.

Ascot Heath is 29 miles southwest of London. I suspect that, in the past, many a young London *bon vivant* tied on his *ascot*, and then journeyed down to Ascot Heath "to tie one on" again.

astrakhan. See **caracul.**

attic/Attic/atticism/Attica/ attic salt/Attic faith

Attic salt is not stored in an *attic,* nor will it give you high blood pressure. All of these featured words are related to the ancient Greek goddess Athena and *Attica,* the land of Athena. We shall start at the top:

attic Originally, *attic* was an architectural style first used in Athens, Greece, in which a small decorative order was placed above a larger order; a story or room directly below the roof of a house. Today, an *attic* is an upright story under a flat roof, while a *garret* is a room under a sloping roof.

Attic of or characteristic of Athens, Greece. Simple elegance; delicate wit.

atticism a graceful phrase.

Attica a region in southeast Greece; a town in western New York State in which there is a state prison.

attic salt graceful, piercing wit.

Attic faith unshakeable faith.

azure

Sangre azul is an old Spanish expression that translates into English as "blue blood," a common phrase applied today to aristocratic people. This colorful expression implied a special ethnic status for those Spaniards who had not intermarried with the darker skinned Moors during the long Moorish occupation of Spain that lasted from 714 to 1492. In the eighteenth century, the people of Castille, proud of their long resistance to the Moors and the purity of their blood, began to use the *sangre azul* phrase. It was a reference to the color of their veins which appeared to be blue against their white skin. It was also an example of ethnic snobbery and racism. The veins of the darker skinned people, who had the blood of the black Moors coursing through their bodies, were neither pronounced nor did they appear blue, and, accordingly, they were not *blue bloods*. The *blue blood* phrase remains in use today, but merely to describe a socially prominent or old-monied person.

The Spanish word for blue, *azul,* the Italian *azzuro,* and the French *azure* can all be traced to the Latin words *lapis lazulus* (*lazuli*), or blue stone. *Lazuli* ultimately is traced to the Persian word *lajward* (*lazward*), itself from the name of the place in Turkestan, according to Ernest Weekley, where the beautiful *lapis lazuli* stones were first found. *Azure* is most often used in prose and poetry to describe a clear blue sky.

On the surface, the color of one person's skin or veins may seem to differ from that of others. Nevertheless, the blood of all humans is, of course, uniformly red. Thus, all humans, not only Americans, are *red-blooded*—an idiom meaning vigorous, lusty, or robust.

BBBBBBBBBBBBB**B**BBBBBBBBBBBBB

babble

Sixty miles south of Baghdad, in modern-day Iraq, are the crumbled mounds of the ancient city of Babylon where, according to the book of Genesis (11:7), the ancient people of Babel once attempted to build a mighty tower (The Tower of Babel) to reach the heavens. But the Lord was not happy with this and "confounded the tongues of the people that they might not understand one another's speech." The result provides us with the English word *babble,* a meaningless confusion of words and sounds.

Babylon, according to language scholars, was in ancient Mesopotamia where the Indo-European family of languages, of which English is a hybrid member, may have started. The moral of this ancient failed project is that things get done on or ahead of schedule when the people involved are willing and able to communicate intelligently and purposefully, and not simply *babble* incoherently.

badminton

The British occupation of India greatly enriched the English language with words like *jodhpur, dumdum, bungalow,* and many more. The English also learned many new sports while in India including the game of *badminton*, but in this case they did not adopt the Indian name for it, *poona*. *Badminton* is a court or lawn game played with light-weight battledores and shuttlecocks.

Battledore was an early word for a racket, and a *shuttlecock* was the missile that was batted back and forth. *Shuttlecock* combines the Anglo-Saxon word *scutel*, meaning missile and is related to the weaver's shuttle because it shoots back and forth. When the cork of the *shuttlecock* was fitted with feathers it resembled a *woodcock* (bird), and the combined result was the thoroughly English word, *shuttlecock*.

Badminton was exported to England by British officials who had served in India. Its English debut in 1873 was at the Duke of Beaufort's place known as *Badminton*, a cozy 10-square-mile estate in the Cotswolds. It was from its early popularity at *Badminton* that the game took its official name.

baldachin

Baghdad is the capital of Iraq. It is an ancient city situated on both banks of the Tigris River with a population today of 2.8 million. It was from this city that the Italians imported a fabric they called *baldachino*. This word was later anglicized to *baldachin* and performed a dual service as the word used to describe the beautiful fabric of Baghdad as well as the special way in which the fabric was applied.

Baldachin fabric was originally a silk brocade interwoven with gold or silver threads. It was apparently so beautiful and expensive that it was reserved mainly for use over the heads of monarchs and church officials. It could be used either as a stationary architectural ornamentation or in a procession. The *baldachin* was part of the pomp and ceremony that helped to create the mystique surrounding monarchs, emperors, and other leaders throughout history. It is still used in Roman Catholic church architecture as well as in papal ceremonies.

balkanization/balkanize/ Finlandization/Vietnamization

Balkanization is defined as the process of dividing a country or territory into small, quarrelsome, ineffective states, and more generally as the process of dividing groups.

The Balkan Peninsula is made up of Albania, Bulgaria, Greece, Romania, most of Yugoslavia, and the European portion of present-day Turkey. The region is named after the Balkan Mountains, which is redundant, since *balkan* is a Turkish word meaning mountain. The Balkan Peninsula comprises an area of 213,000 square miles. Its northern boundary is the Danube and Sava Rivers; the Black Sea and the Sea of Marmara in the east; the Aegean Sea in the south; the Adriatic Sea in the West.

The Balkans are populated with a profusion of small, intensely nationalistic, ethnic groups, which throughout history have been dominated successfully by the Romans, Byzantines, Bulgarians, Serbs, and Ottomans. A series of small wars of independence ensued, followed by a series of wars known as the Balkan Wars. After the First Balkan War in 1913, the great powers supervised the final dismantling of the Turkish (Ottoman) Empire, thus beginning the process now known as *balkanization*.

Two other political terms have been created in the twentieth century built on the *balkanization* model. The first one is *Finlandization* (1969), which William Safire defines as "the process whereby the Soviets intimidate a neighboring non-communist nation into adopting foreign and defense policies of accommodation and acquiescence." *Vietnamization*, the other term coined during the Nixon presidency, refers to a U.S. policy during the Vietnam War of giving the South Vietnamese government responsibility for carrying on the war, thus permitting the eventual withdrawal of the American troops.

ballyhoo/hooey

Ballyhoo is essentially an American word which, when used as a verb, denotes a clamorous and vigorous attempt to win customers or advance any cause; blatant advertising or publicity. As a noun it signifies a clamor or outcry. The source of *ballyhoo* is assumed by some noted authorities to be the town of Ballyhooly in County Cork, Ireland. But the complete origin is a bit more complicated than this toponymous source might suggest. Here is the ballyhoo on *ballyhoo.*

Eric Partridge is one of those who suspect that *ballyhoo* does owe something to the village of Ballyhooly, which is noted for its residents' boisterous debates. But the first element in this focus word, *bally,* is also a euphemism for the British expletive, *bloody,* which itself means fearful, dreadful, terrible, outrageous, and so on. So there is a strong likelihood that *bally* and Ballyhooly combined and fortified each other to create this primarily American English word, *ballyhoo. Ballyhoo* has its own offspring, *hooey,* which means disbelief or nonsense; **buncombe.** It can be traced back to the 1920s.

balmy. See **barmy.**

baloney/bolony/bologna

In the preface of this book are the immortal, but anonymous words, "One should never watch sausages or laws being made." The fact that the quality of sausage meats was, and perhaps still is, suspect is borne out by the use of the word *baloney* to describe a kind of sausage as well as an idiom to mean worthless, nonsense. *Baloney* is an American slang version of the name of a city and province in central Italy, Bologna (pronounced Bolonya). Today, Bologna is known for its excellent cuisine, but at one time this city was best known for its sausage—sausage of Bologna.

This original Bologna product is reputed to have been stuffed with odds and ends, such as chopped guts and seasoned ground meat. The worthless perception of the *baloney* sausage was transferred to anything that was worthless, nonsense, or pure *baloney*. Bologna's name is an evolved version of Bononia, its name in the fourth century B.C. Bononia was named for the people known as the Boii (see **Bohemia**) who settled the area some 2,500 years ago. The first "n" was later changed to "l." Carl Sandburg once wrote, "No matter how you slice it, it's still baloney." This *baloney* etymology, however, is choice "U.S. prime"!

bantam

The word *bantam* is used idiomatically to describe a small but aggressive person. The word was hatched in Bantam, a village in West Java, Indonesia, where a very small fowl was bred especially as a gamecock. This diminutive bird was able to defeat much larger gamecocks, and *bantam* was eventually transferred to describe people that are small but aggressive. In professional boxing, *bantamweight* is a weight class for fighters up to 118 pounds (between flyweight and featherweight).

It is a puzzlement that in order to climb into the pit with a gamecock, a participant must be a chicken. And yet a person who climbs into the ring with a bantamweight is certainly no chicken.

barbarian

The people who live on the north coast of Africa are known in Arabic as *Berbers*. This name can be traced back to an early

Egyptian word for the same people, *Barbar*. The Greeks called them *hoi barbaroi,* literally the stammerers or unintelligibles. Eventually, *barbaroi* was applied to all people other than Greeks or Romans. Later, *barbaroi* was adopted to describe non-Christians as well. The English version, *barbarian,* means a member of a group considered to be primitive, savage.

To the Greeks, the language of the Berbers seemed to be unintelligible stammering, while the language of the Greeks certainly sounded all Greek to the Berbers. Just as the ancient Greeks referred to foreigners as *hoi barbaroi,* today when we don't understand something we say, "It's all Greek to me." I hope this explanation is not Greek to you. The Latin word *barba,* meaning beard, was probably influenced by the beards worn by the Berbers. In this roundabout way we arrived at the English word *barber,* one who cuts hair.

barmy/balmy

St. Mary's of Bethlehem, a sixteenth-century asylum in London, England, has produced several idioms. *Bedlam,* for example, is a corruption of *Bethlehem* that centuries later is still used to describe a place or condition of noise and confusion or insane asylums in general. Surprisingly, or perhaps not so surprisingly, the English slang word *barmy* and its American counterpart, *balmy,* stem from this same world.

According to the late etymologist John Ciardi, the wards at Bedlam were separately named after saints. St. Bartholomew's ward was corrupted by local Londoners to *Barmy,* and the word *barmy* is still defined in British slang as silly or idiotic. *Balmy,* the American version of *barmy,* has the same British slang sense.

Balmy can also mean soothing, mild, and pleasant. This second and more agreeable definition is from *balm,* an aromatic resin originally derived from balsam trees. May your life always be filled with *balmy* days, at least those of the pleasant variety.

Bastille/bastille

On April 23, 1370, construction commenced on a new fortress in Paris which came to be known as the *Bastille*. The project had been authorized by King Charles V of France. The towers of this structure (eight in all) rose 100 feet into the air and the fortress was surrounded by an 80-foot moat. The word *Bastille* is based on the French word *bastide* meaning fortress. Charles V could not have dreamed that 429 years later, the *Bastille*, which had become a symbol of despotism and oppression, would play a central role in the overthrow of the French monarchy on July 14, 1789.

Bastille is also written lower-cased to describe any prison or jail, especially one operated in a tyrannical manner, but it is most frequently used as a literary reference to a prison. July 14 became, and remains today, a French national holiday. On that fateful day back in 1789, the French citizenry were able to enter this impregnable fortress when the gates were opened to allow a detachment of reinforcements to enter. The Parisian mob stormed in along with the soldiers and the fortress fell that same day. French history might have been altered if Charles V had not built the *Bastille* in the fourteenth century, or if the gates of the prison had not been opened on that momentous day in 1789. But great events in history often hinge on such episodes (or gates). In this case, the French monarchy became unhinged by opening the *Bastille's* gates at an inappropriate time.

Bay of Pigs

The course of history has been altered by a number of momentous events. Caesar's crossing the **Rubicon** and Napoleon's defeat at **Waterloo** are two good examples of toponymous watershed incidents. The disastrous *Bay of Pigs* invasion was another one of those significant incidents that had an indirect impact on history. A year later, President John F. Kennedy, bent on recouping U.S. losses, checkmated Nikita Khruschev in a grim game of nuclear chess.

In April of 1961, a group of Cuban exiles, supported and trained by the American military establishment, and with the approval of President John F. Kennedy, attempted an invasion at a bay on the southeast coast of Cuba. The name of this bay is Bahia de Chochino's, or *Bay of Pigs.* At the last minute, President Kennedy reneged on his promise of direct U.S. military support that might have improved the mission's chances of success.

Castro's forces easily defeated the invaders and imprisoned them. One beneficiary of this debacle was the English language, which added a rich new idiom, *Bay of Pigs,* a synonym for **Waterloo** or fiasco.

bayonet

At the confluence of the Nive and Adour Rivers in southwest France is the manufacturing city of Bayonne, center of the Basque people (and the city after which Bayonne, New Jersey, was named). According to tradition, a dagger called a *bayonet* was manufactured there. This first *bayonet* was, of course, named after the city in which it was made in 1490. The name was later used for a knife that was originally inserted into the muzzle of a musket in the sixteenth century. The *bayonet* eventually replaced the long pikes that were used for centuries by European foot soldiers.

It has been said that the American Civil War was the last major war in which hand-to-hand fighting with drawn *bayonets* actually influenced the outcome of battle. Today's soldiers use the *bayonet* as an all-purpose knife, which remains in its scabbard when not in use.

bedlam

In 1242, the Priory (monastery) of St. Mary of Bethlehem was founded in London. Londoners shortened the name of the priory to Bethlehem and this in turn was altered to *Bedlam*. In 1547, the monasteries were dissolved by Henry VIII, and Bedlam was converted into a hospital for the insane, and as such was infamous for the cruel and inhuman treatment meted out to its patients. *Bedlam*, with a small "b," also became a generic term for all insane asylums, and later a place or situation of noisy uproar and confusion.

The Bethlehem from which *bedlam* came is, of course, the small town near Jerusalem where Christ was said to have been born. Bethlehem combines two Semitic elements, *beth* meaning house and *hem* meaning bread (perhaps nut bread) or literally "house of bread." *Beth* was the second letter of the Semitic or Phoenician alphabet upon which the Greek letter Beta (β) was later based. The first element in *bedlam*, *bed*, is therefore simply a reduction from *beth*, later *beta*, and finally *bed*.

Bergamask/bergamsca/bergamot/Bergamo

This is actually a tale of two cities that produced a torrent of toponyms. The two are Bergamo, a city of Lombardy in northern Italy, and Bergama, a town in western Turkey (Asia Minor). The people of Bergamo, Italy, were known as *Bergamasks*. The reputedly awkward manners of these people inspired a dance that is known as a *bergamasca*, a fast dance similar to the **tarantella.**

The word for the Turkish town, Bergama, is a modern version of an ancient region of Turkey known as Pergamum where **parchment** was first made. Bergama is also known for its beautiful *Bergamo* rugs, which are characterized by a long pile with floral or geometric patterns and red-orange hues. The *bergamot* is a small citrus tree that yields a pear-shaped fruit. It is from this fruit that a fragrant essential oil used in making perfume and tea is extracted. The word *bergamot,* in this case, combines the Turkish word *bey,* a word of respect, and *armut,* pear. *Bey armut* was anglicized to *bergamot* because of its phonetic similarity to *Bergamo* and Bergama. There is one final *bergamot,* a European plant, that we shall add to this potpourri of words. It is so named because of its similarity to essence of *bergamot.*

bialy

The *bialy* was probably the inspiration for the popular and more widely known *bagel,* and so I have chosen to trace the origin of both of these Eastern-European-style rolls. And to round out this word platter, I shall also toss in a *blintz,* or at least its origin. While the *blintz* is different from the *bialy* or *bagel,* all three are regionally and alliteratively related and have a distinctly Yiddish flavor.

Our title pastry, *bialy,* is a flat, round baked roll topped with onion flakes. It originated in Bialystok, Poland, an industrial city 105 miles northeast of Warsaw with a population over 200,000. The *bialy* is the only toponym of the trio. The *bagel,* a glazed ring-shaped roll with a tough, chewy texture, is a first cousin of the *bialy* and is derived from the Yiddish word *beygel,* meaning ring.

Our final delicacy, *blintz* (*blihntz*), is a Yiddish version of the Russian word *blinyets,* meaning little pancakes. It is a crepe filled with cheese, potato, or fruit and then baked or fried.

bible/Bible

The word for "The Good Book" is actually older than the *Bible* itself. In fact, the *Bible* was named after an ancient city that had little to do with the actual writing of the *Bible*. Here is the chapter and verse on the origin of this book.

The Phoenicians, a Semitic tribe that lived in what is now Lebanon and Syria, were the greatest merchants of the eastern Mediterranean lands. Among their most important items of trade was the papyrus, which they converted into writing materials at Byblos, an ancient port city in present-day Lebanon that is now called Jubayl. This early form of paper was given the name *biblios* by the Greeks after the city from which it was exported to the world. *Biblion* later came to mean a little book.

In the fourth century A.D., the Greeks began calling the holy Christian book the *Bible*. The word *bible*, when lower-cased, can be any book or other source considered to be an authority in its field.

Big Apple, The

New York is definitely a big-league city (Yankees, Mets, Giants, Jets, Knicks, Rangers) and, as such, deserves a big league *apple-ation*. At the core of *The Big Apple* idiom is one of the early centers of jazz.

According to *Safire's Political Dictionary*, Cab Calloway defined *Apple* as the "big town, the main stem, Harlem." Safire indicates that, in a 1976 interview with this great jazz band leader, Mr. Calloway explained further that *The Big Apple*, the name of a Harlem night club in the mid-1930s, was a **mecca** for jazz musicians. The name of that club was eventually adopted as a nickname for New York City by jazz performers and afficionados.

The Big Apple name did not fall upon the city on the Hudson until the mid 1970s. At that time, the New York City Convention and Visitors Bureau, tiring of the "Fun City" nickname, reached down into the deep barrel of New York's rich history and culture and pulled out this *appletising* name for the greatest city on earth.

bikini

Two very explosive incidents occurred in 1946 within five days of each other. At the time, these two events had a powerful impact on mankind.

On July 1, 1946, the United States detonated an atomic bomb on the tiny atoll (reef) of Bikini in the Pacific Marshall Islands. Four days later, on July 5, a French fashion designer, Louis Reard, introduced a very daring two-piece bathing suit. According to *The Second World Almanac Book of Invention*, this garment was made of cotton fabric and was printed with press clippings.

Reard gave the name *bikini* to his creation because he suspected that it might have the same psychological effect on men that the A-bomb explosion had on the atoll. And while the bomb's nuclear fallout has long since stopped, the *bikini's* fallout continues to this day.

billingsgate

The break in at the Watergate complex in Washington, D.C. in the early 1970s proved to be President Richard M. Nixon's **Waterloo.** This event opened up the floodgates that released a torrent of new words fashioned after Watergate and employing the "-gate" suffix as a code element for the newest federal scandal, such as, Irangate and Contragate. Another word with the "-gate" suffix, *billingsgate*, figured peripherally in the Watergate incident.

Billingsgate is an English idiom that means a deluge of foul-mouthed, abusive language. Although sailors and porters are known for their "salty" use of expletives, they could not hold a candle to the men and women who worked at the *Billingsgate* fish market in London, England, when it came to swearing. The use of *billingsgate* in this way can be pursued back to the mid-seventeenth century. The gate itself can be traced back to a much earlier date. In fact, *Billingsgate* first appeared in print in the thirteenth century. *Billingsgate,* along with Ludgate, was among the many early gates to the ancient town of London. *Billingsgate* is a contraction of *Belins* and *gate*. Belin was thought to be a son of King Lud, a mythical founder of London (Lud's hill).

What surprised many people about Dick Nixon's Watergate tapes was the liberal use of *billingsgate* language by the president and his associates.

blarney

In 1602, an Irishman by the name of Cormack McCarthy sweet-talked the British, who had encircled his castle, into delaying its takeover indefinitely. This historic event occurred in Blarney, near Cork, Ireland. McCarthy's smooth talk subsequently resulted in the toponym *blarney,* meaning smooth, flattering talk.

If you journey to the Emerald Isle and visit the ruins of Blarney Castle, you will be introduced to the legend of its stone. This famous stone is positioned in such a way that tourists must get on their backs and lean out over the parapet in order to buss the Blarney stone. Legend has it that great skill in flattery will be bestowed on those who participate in this uncomfortable exercise. It is said, however, that if you refuse to kiss this well-worn stone it will fall upon you. You can take it from this author, who visited Blarney Castle and kissed the stone, that the legend is just so much *blarney,* which also means nonsensical talk.

blighty. See **English.**

bohemian

Bohemia is a region of Czechoslovakia occupying an area the size of Ohio. For much of its history, it was an independent kingdom. The name of this place came from a Celtic people of Gaul, the *Boii,* who settled there in 400 B.C.

A *Bohemian* is a resident of *Bohemia,* but the word has been lower-cased to describe an artist, writer, or simply a vagabond who lives free of social conventions. This characterization was, for the most part, due to the mistaken French notion that these people were Gypsies.

The **Gypsy** association was further established in many literary references from Shakespeare to Thackeray. The latter of these two great English authors described Becky Sharp in *Vanity Fair* thus: "She has a wild, roving nature, inherited from her father and mother, who were both Bohemians by taste and circumstances." The poor starving artist portrayal was fixed in La Boheme, the beautiful opera about artists by Puccini.

The use of *bohemian* to describe a vagabond has been replaced over the years by such words as *beatnik, hippie,* and so on. The desire to be free of societal restrictions continues to be an attractive alternative for some, and the need to create new names for themselves is also strong.

bohunk/Canuck/gringo/ Chicano

Most ethnic slurs start out quite innocently as harmless nicknames for the national origins of immigrants. Some of these terms become widely used and, in some cases, are highly offensive to their targets. The degree to which an aspersion becomes objectionable depends, it would seem, on whether it is enunciated by a minority or a majority. The majority groups are less sensitive because they are, after all, the majority. Here is a medley from our quiver of toponymous ethnic slurs, most of which have lost their sting.

bohunk came from the Chicago steel mills and coal mines, and apparently combines *(bo)hemian* and *(Hung)arian.* During World War II, it was directed toward all foreigners in the Windy City. **Honky** is also derived from *Hungarian*.

Canuck is a Canadian and unites *Canadian* and *Chinook*, the name of an Indian tribe that lived on the Columbia River and traded with the Hudson Bay traders.

gringo in South America *gringo* means a foreigner, especially a North American or an Englishman. *Gringo* appears to be an alteration of the Spanish word *Griego,* a Greek. The "n" in *gringo* was probably borrowed from the "n" in English. So *gringo* originally described someone, probably a supervisor or landowner, who did not speak Spanish, but rather English or some other language—"They all sound *Griego* to me!"

Chicano is derived from the ending of the word *Mexicano* which the Aztecs pronounced Meshicano.

Polak see **Polka.**

This etymologist frankly doesn't care what you call me as long as it is not an *entomologist* (one who studies insects), because that really bugs me.

Bombay duck

There is something fishy about *Bombay duck,* a dish that originated in India but which has nothing whatsoever to do with fowl. *Bombay,* in this case, is another example of false (or folk) etymology, a popular but false notion of the origin of a word. This culinary specialty is also called *bummalo duck*. Both *Bombay* and *bummalo* are derived from, and are perversions of, a native Indian word *bombila,* the name of a lizard fish that is commonly found in the rivers of Asia including those of India.

The *bombila* was exported from Bombay. It was heavily flavored with chutney and Indian spices and served as a substitute for roast duck. Therefore, *Bombay duck* is in the same category as **Welsh rabbit,** a dish of melted cheese served on toast, and *Cape Cod Turkey,* codfish. The names of all three are often used satirically for a food specialty that most people could not afford for one that they could afford, according to the *Morris Dictionary of Word and Phrase Origins* by William and Mary Morris. The name *Bombay duck* became a euphemism for anything a person could not afford.

boondocks/boonies

This thoroughly American-sounding idiom, *the boondocks,* actually comes all the way from the Philippine Islands, an archipelago consisting of 7,100 islands (4,327 remain unnamed) in southwest Asia. In the Tagalog language of the Philippines, *bundok* means mountain.

The first westerner to discover these islands was the Portuguese navigator Ferdinand Magellan (1480–1521), who was also the first man to circumnavigate the earth. He proved that the earth was round, but he did it for Spain, not Portugal. Spain, therefore, controlled these islands until 1898 when they came under U.S. control as a result of the treaty with the Spanish that ended the Spanish American War.

The U.S. forces picked up on the word *bundok,* which they also referred to as the outback. *Bundok* was later Americanized to the *boondocks,* an uninhabited area with thick natural vegetation, such as a back woods or marsh. It is now used to describe a remote rural area; the sticks; the dumps. The *boonies,* an economy-sized version of *boondocks,* entered the language in 1965.

If you must go to the *boonies,* we suggest that you do so accompanied by *a boon companion,* one who is jovial or convivial. Our bonus word, *boon,* comes via the French word *bon* from the Latin word *bonus*, meaning good, which is what a bonus usually is.

Boston, banned in/ Boston Brahmin/ Boston baked beans

The name of the city of Boston, Massachusetts, was transported by the English settlers to the New World from the Boston in Lincolnshire, England. The Lincolnshire Boston, a much smaller edition (population 27,000), was named after St. Botolph's stone, the site of St. Botolph's Christian missionary. Some hold that the "*-ston*" element was a stone church, but all agree that *St. Boltolph's stone* was contracted to *Boston*. Fortunately (or unfortunately), this book was not *banned in Boston*, one of several interesting Boston idioms.

Boston, banned in During the roaring twenties, the mayor of Boston empowered the Watch and Ward Society (WWS) to ban books from sale in Boston, Massachusetts, in order to protect the morals of the people of that city. It is widely reported that the chief censor, an injured musician who was no longer able to play in a burlesque band, was also the mayor's cousin. Publishers sought to have their books banned in Boston because of the positive impact such a distinction had on the sales of a book. The WWS lost its power shortly after it was challenged by U.S. writer, editor, and critic H.L. Mencken.

Boston Brahmin In 1860, Oliver Wendell Holmes wrote that, "He comes of the Brahmin caste of New England. This is the harmless, inoffensive, untitled aristocracy." A *Brahmin* is a member of India's highest caste. This phrase often is used disparagingly of the oldest and most prominent of Boston family members.

Boston baked beans One of Boston's nicknames is *"Beantown,"* a name bestowed upon it because of the Bostonian fondness for baked beans. It is widely accepted that the early English settlers to Boston obtained a recipe for sweetened baked beans from the local Indians. It later became a favorite weekend repast with the Puritans of the city who observed the Sabbath's no-work rules. As a result, baked beans became a Saturday night ritual with many Bostonians. The beans not consumed on Saturday would be reheated on Sunday, often by the local baker who would deliver them, along with his baked brown bread, for the main Sabbath meal.

Bowery, the/Bowery boy/ Bowery bum

The following lyrics are from an 1891 musical entitled *A Trip to Chinatown* written by Hoyt and Gaunt:

> The Bow'ry, the Bow'ry!
> They say such things, and
> they do strange things. On
> the Bow'ry, the Bow'ry.
> I'll never go there any more!

Today, the *Bowery* is a New York City street that extends from Chatham Square to East Fourth Street, noted for cheap hotels and saloons, and peopled by the destitute and homeless. (Unfortunately, the last part of this definition describes a lot of other neighborhoods in today's **Big Apple.**) The *Bowery boy,* a rough or rowdy type who inhabited the area in the mid-nineteenth century, has given way to the *Bowery bum,* a person who lives on the street.

The name *Bowery* comes from the Dutch word *bowerij,*

meaning a farm. The land where this street now rests was part of a farm or *bowerij* that was purchased by Peter Stuyvesant in 1631 for 6,400 guilders. In the 1670s, it was a popular rural area for summer picnics.

Not too much has changed on the *Bow'ry* since the above lyrics were written, and not too many people go to the *Bowery* any more unless, of course, they are looking for lamps, restaurant supplies, or are just plain down on their luck. One thing is certain, though: today's *Bowery* is, sadly, no picnic.

Bristol fashion/Bristol milk/ Bristols

The English, a great naval power beginning with their victory over the Spanish Armada in 1588, were also noted for the A–1 (a Lloyd's of London vessel rating initiated in Edward Lloyd's coffee shop in seventeenth-century London) condition of their ships. Bristol, an English seaport on the Avon River in southwest England, was a major center of this shipping activity. It was from Bristol that John Cabot departed on the voyage that led to the discovery of Nova Scotia and Newfoundland.

As a center of naval activity and efficiency, *Bristol* became synonymous with "good order" in expressions such as *shipshape and Bristol fashion* or simply *Bristol fashion*. Of earlier vintage was the idiom *Bristol milk* which, though somewhat archaic, was a satirical metaphor for the sherry wine that was imported to the port of Bristol.

Bristols is a British toponym for female breasts. This slang curiosity, as is so often the case, can be traced to a Cockney rhyming slang, in this case, "Bristol city rhymes with titty." In Cockney slang, the first word of the rhyme becomes synonymous with the last word of the verse, in this case, titty.

British. See **English.**

Broadway/off Broadway/ off-off-Broadway

It is said that *Broadway* is the longest street in the world. Starting at Bowling Green in lower Manhattan, it continues north all the way into the city of Yonkers in Westchester County. *Broadway* is best known, however, for an eight-block stretch between 42nd and 50th Streets. This special section of *Broadway* is called the theater district or The Great White Way, because of the theaters and bright lights characteristic of the area. Today, most of the legitimate theaters are not on *Broadway* but off its interesting side streets instead. Other New York legitimate theaters that are truly *off Broadway* deserve mention here as well. Since World War II, professional drama groups distinguished by experimental productions began to pop up in other parts of the city. These minitheaters became known by the general term *off Broadway*. One of the first *off Broadway* theaters was the Circle in the Square. *Off Broadway* theaters do not exceed 299 seats and are granted special concessions by theater unions. The term *off Broadway* first appeared in print in 1953. Smaller yet, and even more experimental than *off Broadway*, is *off-off-Broadway (OOB)*, a term that first appeared in print in 1967.

Broadway has also come to mean tawdry or garish because of its bright lights, pimps, prostitutes, and XXX-rated movies. *Broadway* was also the nickname of a New York Jets star quarterback, Joe Namath, who reportedly liked the "bright lights" of *Broadway*.

Brobdingnagian. See **Lilliputian.**

Bronx cheer

In 1641 Jhonas (Jonas) Broncs (Bronck) purchased a large farm from the Indians. His farm later came to be known as the

Bronck's farm. It is the only one of the five New York City boroughs that is usually preceded by "The." This is probably due to the fact that the borough was once privately owned; a person visiting Jonas and his family would be visiting the Broncs, in the same way one might say that he is visiting the Joneses.

The *Bronx cheer* idiom, which first appeared in print in 1929, is a loud abrasive noise made by placing the tongue between the lips and blowing. This *cheer* is not a cheer at all, but an expression of contempt or derision. The *Bronx cheer* is synonymous with *raspberries* (*razzberries;* also *razz*), a British term from Cockney rhyming slang (raspberry tart rhymes with fart). One additional synonym for the *Bronx cheer* is *the bird*, as in to give someone *the bird*. *The bird* is a hissing sound made by geese that is similar in sound to the *Bronx cheer*. While it might be natural to assume that the *Bronx cheer* was developed at Yankee Stadium, a baseball park located in the Bronx, according to Stuart Berg Flexner this is not the case. Why this rude echoic sound should be associated with the name of this borough remains a mystery. Perhaps the *Bronx cheer* is simply a crude rendition of the word *Bronx*.

brummagem

Birmingham is a city of nearly one million people in the West Midlands of England with a lustrous, if not illustrious, manufacturing past. It was an important town even back in the days when the Romans, who called it Bremenium, were in control of the British Isles. A much later name, or nickname, for this industrial center was *Brummagem*, which at first was an affectionate term, but later became a synonym for something worthless or very inferior; cheap or showy. We shall trace the rise and fall of this toponymous "gem," *brummagem*.

A *groat* (meaning great) was a silver coin of the realm minted between 1227 and 1662. In the early seventeenth century, counterfeit groats worth four pennies were made in Birmingham and, as a result, were called *brummagems*. Because of the bogus nature of these coins, *brummagem* took on the added sense of sham; not genuine.

With this reputation for producing lustrous counterfeits going for it, Birmingham later developed a reputation for manufacturing cheap and flashy jewelry and gems for peddlers. This junk jewelry also came to be named *brummagem* after its place of origin. Today, *brummagem* has become generalized as a synonym for anything showy, inferior, or worthless. Back in its junk jewelry heyday, one might have asked, "Is that a genuine gem?" The reply to this query might have been, "No, that's a *brummaGEM!*"

buckram

Bukhara is a territory in the central Asian region of the Soviet Union. This agricultural district has figured in the story of **paisley,** but is best known for a kind of cotton grown there that goes by the English name *buckram*. *Buckram* is a coarse cotton fabric heavily sized with glue, used for stiffening garments and bookbindings. At an earlier time, Bukhara was noted for the beautiful hand embroidered shawls produced there. *Buckram*, like so many other fabrics, has become a metaphor for human behavior, and is used to describe someone who is stiff in manner, extremely precise, or formal. Other examples of fabric metaphors include *cotton to*, be friendly with; *bombast*, padded speech; **sleazy,** vulgar, disreputable.

Buckram should not be confused with *buckra*, a white man or boss. *Buckra* was introduced by African slaves working on antebellum plantations of the U.S. South, and is derived from the Efik language of southeastern Nigeria.

bungalow

English-speaking people are the world's most prolific word pilferers, a process politely referred to in linguistic circles as "borrowing." As a result of England's occupation of India, which started in the mid-eighteenth century and lasted for 200 years, the English language has absorbed many Indian (Hindi) words. English control over India lasted until this Asian nation became an independent dominion in the British Commonwealth of Nations on August 15, 1947. One nineteenth-century source, according to *The Story of English,* listed 26,000 Indian words that at the time had been incorporated into English. *Bungalow* is among those borrowings.

The Indian word *bangla* literally means "of Bengal," a former Indian province in northeast British India. *Bangla,* which was anglicized to *bungalow,* described a one-storied thatched or tiled home, usually surrounded by a *veranda,* another English borrowing from the Hindi language defined as a porch or balcony, usually roofed and often partly enclosed, extending along the outside of a building.

The *bungalow* was very popular in the United States in the early twentieth century. It was normally one and one-half stories high and had a wide gabled roof, a multiwindowed dormer, and was frequently built of rustic materials.

Bungalows were often constructed as do-it-yourself projects, and accordingly, they were often bungled (from the Swedish word *bengla,* meaning to work ineffectually).

bunk/buncombe

What Felix Walker did for Buncombe County, North Carolina, was certainly not calculated to win him any awards from the local Chamber of Commerce. Five words spoken by him during the Missouri Compromise Slavery Debates in 1819 made the name of this particular county, which was part of his congressional district, a term synonymous with nonsense. How did this public relations disaster occur? Herein lies the tale.

Felix Walker, who represented Buncombe County, a mountain district in North Carolina, was known for making irrelevant speeches in Congress. The primary purpose of his orations appeared to be to get on the record so that his constituents would feel that they were being well represented. These speeches rarely addressed the questions at hand.

Accordingly, when Walker rose to speak during a critical phase of these slavery-related debates, his fellow party members urged him to be silent. Undaunted, Felix Walker started his speech by saying, "I must speak for Buncombe."

This harmless phrase apparently captured the essence of what Felix's speeches were all about, "nonsense," which they equated with the man from *Buncombe*. Within ten years, *buncombe* was accepted as a standard dictionary word with the first letter lower-cased.

Bunkum is another acceptable spelling for *buncombe*, while *bunk* is a shortened form of the word. To *debunk* is to take the foolishness out of something and that, of course, is no bunk!

byzantine

The *Byzantine* Empire held its power in the eastern Mediterranean for 1,130 years during the Middle Ages, and was well known for its complex political structure. Therefore, *byzantine* came to mean relating to, or characterized by intrigue, scheming; highly complicated, intricate, and involved.

The Empire extended from Mesopotamia to Sardinia and Sicily and included Asia Minor, Greece, and the southern Slovak states of Bulgaria, Croatia, and Serbia. The art, architecture, and indeed the entire culture of that vast region was heavily influenced by the *Byzantine* domination. This empire was started by Constantine I, called the Great, the first Roman Emperor to become a Christian. He was proclaimed emperor at Eboracum (York) in Britain when his father Constantius died.

Constantine eventually transferred the Roman Empire from Rome to the site of ancient Byzantium on the Bosporus and renamed it Constantinople on A.D. May 11, 330. The Greek word *buzan* meant close-pressed and perhaps the ancient word influenced the name of that densely populated city. While this city changed its name again in 1930 to Istanbul, said to be a Turkish corruption of Constantinople, it remains *byzantine* to this day.

ccccccccccCcccccccccc

Cajun

The origin of the word *Cajun* is an archetypal lesson in the closely paralleled relationship between etymology and history.

When the English obtained the area now known as Nova Scotia from the French, it was called *Acadia,* a Micmac Indian name for the region. In 1755, faced with imminent war with France, the British decided to deport the potentially dangerous 10,000 French Acadians living there to new locations ranging from Maine to Louisiana.

While *Acadian* was used to describe all of these French deportees, the word has been corrupted to *Cajun* and, today, refers particularly to those Acadians who settled in Louisiana, and to persons related to a Louisianian of Acadian ancestry. *Cajun* is also used to describe a French dialect of Louisiana and spicy foods native to that area.

The sad story of the Acadian deportation is captured in Longfellow's immortal poem, *Evangeline—A Tale of Acadia*. Perhaps you recall its haunting opening lines:

> "This is the forest primeval.
> The murmuring pines and the hemlock . . ."

calico

T.S. Eliot's *Old Possum's Book of Practical Cats* includes this verse from a poem entitled "Naming Cats":

> The naming of Cats is a difficult matter
> It isn't just one of your holiday games
>
> You may think at first I'm as mad as a hatter
> When I tell you, a cat must have three different names.

Eliot's children's verses about cats were the source of Andrew Lloyd Weber's musical, *Cats.* One descriptive name for a cat not included in Eliot's verses is the *calico,* a domestic cat, almost always a female, with a variegated black, white, and orange coloring. *Calico* is an anglicized version of the French word *calicot,* a fine cotton cloth originally imported from Calcutta, India, beginning in the sixteenth century. Calcutta is on the Malibar coast of northeast India. *Calico* cloth was later printed with a figured pattern and became a fairly common fabric. The variegated patterns that became associated with *calico* cloth were later used to describe a cat of similar coloring, as well as certain species of aquatic life such as the *calico clam, calico crab,* and *calico oyster*.

According to Eliot's verse, one must provide three names for a cat. We have supplied one name, that is if your cat happens to be of the spotted or *calico* type. But you must provide the other two. You may even wish to use the name Jellicle as Eliot did. For other intriguing names we recommend that you get a copy of *Old Possum's Practical Book of Cats* at your library.

cambric/chambray/cambric tea

In the thirteenth century, a weaver named Batiste, according to legend, was the first person to manufacture a thin white sheer cloth in Kameryk, a textile center which at the time was in Flanders. Batiste's name is still associated with this kind of fabric, which is still known as *batiste.* In 1678, Kameryk was ceded to France and has since become known as *Cambrai. Cambrai* continued to be the center of manufacture for a similar type of fabric which is also known as *cambrai,* a thin, plain cotton or linen fabric having a fine close weave that is usually white. American English wove its own alteration of *cambrai, chambray,* which is used to describe a fine gingham fabric.

Cambric tea is an American idiom for a beverage served to children in lieu of the adults' more potent tea. It consists of hot water, milk, sugar, and often a small amount of tea. This tea substitute was the equivalent of the *Shirley Temple,* a cocktail without alcohol served to children while the grown-ups were drinking a stronger beverage. *Cambric tea* is so called because, like *cambric* fabric, it was thin, white, and lacked the substance of real tea. *Cambric tea* can also be used as a metaphor for anything that is bland and lacking in excitement.

Camelot

Camelot has obviously had the benefit of very good "press" over the centuries, and as a result it is used to refer to any idyllic place or period, especially one of great happiness. The original *Camelot* was a city ruled by the legendary King Arthur and his Knights of the Round Table. *Camelot's* most recent use was in connection with Washington, D.C., in the early 1960s during the administration of President John F. Kennedy. We are a bit skeptical about how idyllic these two *Camelots* actually were. After all, King Arthur's most trusted knight, Sir Launcelot, had an affair with Arthur's wife Guenevere. And recent reports of President Kennedy's sexual escapades while in the White House suggest that his twentieth-century version of *Camelot* was also not without problems.

The original legend of King Arthur was passed down by

minstrels and storytellers. According to some sources, the story of King Arthur may have been based on a real British King of the sixth century A.D. who bravely resisted the invasions of the Germanic tribes. During the Kennedy era, a musical entitled *Camelot* appeared on **Broadway** and, at the time, some people compared the glamorous outward appearance of the Kennedy presidency with King Arthur's Court. Perhaps Kennedy's Court was similar to that of King Arthur's after all—they both had their share of courtesans.

canary/canary yellow

The Canary Islands, which are in the Atlantic Ocean 60 miles off the coast of northwest Africa, gave birth to a beautiful songbird loved the world over. The 13 islands in this Spanish chain were not named after these popular pets, however, but for the dogs that proliferated the islands. It was the ancient nautical visitors to the islands who actually named them the Canaria, derived from the Latin word for dog, *canis*.

Because of this bird's talent for singing, *canary* is also used idiomatically to describe a police informer.

Cannae

Although *Cannae* is a rarely used word, it is worthy of inclusion in this book if only because it evokes the fascinating story of one of history's greatest generals and his most famous victory. *Cannae* (pronounced cānee) was an ancient town in Apulia, Italy, near modern Barletta where Hannibal (247–183 B.C.) defeated the Roman army on August 2, 216 B.C.. It was the Roman army's greatest single defeat.

Hannibal was the son of another great general of Carthage. His father made the boy swear an oath as a youth to always hate Rome. Young Hannibal became a general at the age of 25, and was highly successful in most of his battles with Rome. The most famous, perhaps, was his defeat of the Romans at *Cannae*. In that great battle, Hannibal formed his Carthaginian army of 40,000 men in a semicircle. When the Romans attacked its center, it yielded while the two flanks surrounded the Romans. This tactic is called the *double envelopment* and is used in modern warfare. At *Cannae*, the Carthaginians killed 50,000 Romans and captured another 10,000. *Cannae* has come to mean any critical battle that is a turning point of a great general's career. **Waterloo,** which was Napolean's *Cannae,* has also become a metaphor for the turning point in many another career. Hannibal was hounded by the Romans for his *perfida Punica* (see **Punic faith**). He finally committed suicide when the Romans demanded his surrender in 183 B.C.

cannibal

Sometimes the name for an entire people becomes synonymous with the peculiar practices of a few of its members. *Cannibal,* one who eats human flesh, is an example of a tribal name, as well as a placename that was so immortalized.

The Caniba and Carib Indians were brought to the attention of the world by Christopher Columbus. These Indians, who inhabited Cuba and other islands of the area, were suspected of eating human flesh. The Caribs gave their name to the Caribbean Islands, while the assumed man-eating proclivities of the Canibas eventually led to the *cannibal* word.

Canossa

Inheriting a kingdom at the age of six can cause a person to become very self-centered and used to getting his own way. Such was probably the case with King Henry IV (1050–1106) who became king of the Holy Roman Empire when he was just six years old. In 1075, Henry came in conflict with Pope Gregory VII over church appointments. When Henry could not get his way over the issue, he simply held a council at Worms and fired the pope. The pope, however, refused to take this sitting down and countered by excommunicating the king. The pope's action had the effect of releasing Henry's subjects from the king's authority.

Two years later, in January 1077, Henry, having lost the early rounds of this skirmish, literally got cold feet when he humbled himself before the pope's castle. This occurred at *Canossa* in northern Italy where the pope was residing at the time. Legend has it that for his penance, Henry actually stood barefoot and bareheaded in the snow outside the pope's castle for three days until the pontiff received him. As a result of this incident, *Canossa* has become a metaphor for a place or a scene of great humiliation. Henry was finally forgiven by the pope who restored him to the sanctity of the church. This enabled him to regain absolute control over his people. But, as Lord Acton once observed, "absolute power corrupts absolutely," and in 1084 Henry won the final round when he fired the pope for the last time. You really cannot blame the king for being mad at the pope, though. Nobody likes to be "left out in the cold."

cantaloupe/cantaloup

The *cantaloupe* is a variety of melon, *cucumis melo cantalupensis*, of the gourd family, having a hard, scaly, and warty rind, and chiefly grown in Europe. This delicious fruit was first grown in Armenia. In the early eighteenth century, however, this melon was introduced and first cultivated in Europe at Castle Cantalupo, a papal estate near Rome. The name of Cantalupo became associated with this tasty new fruit.

The source of this placename, Cantalupo, is quite old and combines the Latin words *cantar*, to sing, and *loupus*, wolf; literally, singing wolf. *Cantaloupes* are also known as muskmelons. In the United States, the *cantaloupe* applies to just one variety of muskmelon, a small (two to four pound), round to oval, heavily netted, and highly perishable variety. Melon, incidentally, is derived from the Greek word *melon*, meaning apple.

canter

One of the first settlements established by the Anglo-Saxon invaders of Britain was Canterbury, a name derived from the Anglo-Saxon words *cant weir burig*, which literally translates as the hill or fort of the men of the border. Canterbury, in the southeast corner of England, is a charming place to visit.

Indeed, centuries later, many religious pilgrims from all over England and Europe would ride on horseback along the old Kent (originally Cant) road on their way to the Shrine of St. Thomas à Becket, located in Canterbury Cathedral. The slow, easy gallop adopted by the pilgrims was called a *Canterbury gallop*, which was eventually shortened to *canter*.

The *canter* was a faster pace than the one set by the pilgrims to the Holy Land, who were said to *saunter*. Some etymologists believe that this slow-paced word, *saunter*, came from the Latin *Sainte Terra* meaning "Holy Land." *Saunter* currently means to roam or loiter.

Canuck. See **bohunk**.

capitol

It is of *capital* (foremost) importance that one understand the difference between *capital* and *capitol*. Despite the fact that both words stem from the same source, they have quite different meanings now. We shall explore the origin of *capital* as well as the historical legend that created its homophone, *capitol*.

The two words stem from the Latin word *caput* and its cognate *capitalis* both meaning the head. Its English version, *capital*, has a variety of meanings, including the top of a column, wealth, the city or town serving as the seat of a government, and an indication that something is excellent.

Capitol, however, is limited to just one meaning: the building in which a state's legislature assembles. The Congress of the United States is referred to as Capitol Hill because the U.S. Capitol building is situated on a hill in our nation's capital. The origin of *capitol* is the Latin word *capitoleum*, the name of the Temple of Jupiter that stood on the Capitoline Hill in ancient Rome. Legend has it that a human head (*caput*) was discovered during the excavation of its foundation, and some say the structure derived its name from this event.

Caracul. See **karakul.**

caryatid

Those readers who have been to Greece have undoubtedly journeyed to the top of the Acropolis in Athens to observe and enjoy the breathtaking architecture of the Parthenon, Erectheum, and other structures of this high city (*acro*, high, and *polis*, city). The Erectheum, a smallish temple, is unique among the buildings of this acropolis because of its *caryatids*, or supporting columns carved in the form of draped female figures. All such architectural forms are now called *caryatids*.

The female figures depicted in these columns are a reference to the dance of the virgins at the festival held in the ancient temple of Artemis Caryatids at Caryae, a town of Laconia (see **laconic**) on the Peloponnesus peninsula in Greece. The original virgins supporting the Erectheum Temple were found to be losing their structural virtue several years ago. So, in order to preserve the purity, so to speak, of these pristine *caryatids* and protect them from further assaults of the highly corrosive Athens air, the virgins were removed from the Erectheum and replaced with concrete replicas. Although virgins are not always easy to find nowadays, the Caryae maidens of the Erectheum can still be seen in the National Museum of Archeology in downtown Athens where they now reside.

cashmere

High up in the rarified air of the Himalayas of Tibet and mountainous regions of India lives a special breed of goat, the *Kashmir*, or *Cashmere*. The name of this goat was taken from the former princely Indian state of Kashmir. This long-haired goat is famous for its fine, silky wool. It is actually the fine downy wool at the roots of its hair that is so highly prized. The average Cashmere goat's annual fleece yield is a (cash)*mere* three ounces, which explains the high cost of this kind of wool. The most highly prized goats of this variety are from the highest regions where their coats are yellow as opposed to the pure white Cashmeres in the lower altitudes.

Cashmere is lower-cased when referring to the wool of this animal as well as garments (sweaters, dresses, and scarves) made from it. In the early nineteenth century, beautifully designed hand-woven shawls made of and in Kashmir became the rage in Europe. These *cashmeres* were so popular that the hand loom weavers of Paisley, Scotland, produced lower priced "knock-offs" of the original *cashmere* shawls. The *cashmere* designs, interpreted by the **Paisley** weavers, resulted in the beautiful fabric designs currently so popular.

caucasian

Caucasian, with a capital "C," simply denotes a person or persons of the Caucasus region of the Soviet Union which is between the Black and Caspian Seas. In its lower-case version, *caucasian* is defined more generally as a person or division of humankind exemplified by fair to dark skin, straight to tightly curled hair, and light to very dark eyes, originally living in Europe, parts of North Africa, western Asia, and India. And while this division is no longer used by the scientific community, it is still in common use today.

It was Johann Blumenbach (1752–1840), a German physiologist and comparative anatomist, who divided all humankind into five divisions: Caucasian, Mongolian, American (Indian), Ethiopian, and Malayan. He chose the people of the Caucasus as an example of the *caucasian* (white) race because it is said that he admired the women of that region. (Cherchez la femme!) A more appropriate name for that division might have been the *European geographical race,* but that just doesn't seem to have the same bite to it as *caucasian*. Blumenbach's theories are now considered to be unscientific and somewhat racist, but they remain in use because of a lack of a better system of classification.

Chambray. See **cambric.**

Champs Elysees. See **Elysian.**

Chantilly

Jiles "Big Bopper" Richardson used *Chantilly lace* in his big hit, *Chantilly Lace* (1958) to describe "what he liked" in the way of girls.

> Chantilly Lace and a pretty face
> And a pony tail hanging down
> A wiggle in her walk and a

giggle in her talk makes
the world go round . . .
Oh baby that's what I like.

The source of this frilly lace was the beautiful town of Chantilly (population 10,500) which lies 25 miles north of Paris, France, in the province of Oise. In the nineteenth century, it was known for the manufacture of *Chantilly lace,* a delicate lace, in black or white, scalloped along one edge and often having a design of scrolls, vases, or baskets of flowers. It is widely used, even today, for bridal and evening gowns. In the nineteenth century, every woman's wardrobe included a black or white *Chantilly* shawl.

Chantilly was also the inspiration for a decorative dessert topping of cream formerly whipped up in Chantilly. It was piped onto cakes and strawberries in a way that was reminiscent of scalloped lace. Currently, the town of Chantilly is best known for its fourteenth-century chateau and annual horse races.

Chantilly Lace was the "Bopper's" first and only hit song. He was killed in a plane crash along with Ritchie Valens and Buddy Holly on February 3, 1959.

charlatan

The town of Cerreto, Italy, was the source of the word *charlatan,* a person who pretends to have expert knowledge or skill that he or she does not actually possess. *Charlatan* has undergone several changes in spelling and meaning since its conception as *cerratanus,* a seller of papal indulgences at Cerreto. Apparently, trade in these religious favors was a major industry in that town during the Middle Ages.

Later, as *ciaratano,* it described a patent medicine salesman of Cerreto; a quack. Eventually, he plied his wares throughout Italy. In the twentieth century, patent medicine men were almost entirely put out of business by agencies such as the Food and Drug Administration (FDA) and the word was broadened to its modern definition.

The word *quack*, generally associated with fake medical practitioners, is a shortened version of *quacksalver*, a word that combines the Old Norse word *kvaka*, one who prattles about his salves, with *salves* (medicines). *Charlatans* or *quacks* may have a soothing manner, but they certainly do not have a patent on reliable salves or cures.

Charleston

The *Charleston* is a vigorous rhythmic ballroom dance that was named after Charleston, South Carolina, where this very physical dance was born. *Charleston* was founded in 1670 and named in honor of King Charles II of England. Originally called Charlestown, in 1783 its name was shortened to *Charleston*.

In the 1920s the *Charleston* dance craze started, and by 1923 a song, *Charleston*, written by C. Mack and J. Johnson was published and became closely associated with this popular dance. The *Encyclopedia Brittanica* states that the *Charleston* is "an informal dance of American Negro origins." It may have originated with African tribal dances and was further defined on the plantations of the South. It is believed that tap dancing also originated on southern plantations. It is presumed that the lively 4/4 time of the Charleston influenced the jitterbug dance of the 1940s, which in turn, inspired Rock 'n' Roll a decade later.

Chartreuse/chartreuse/ Charterhouse

Most wines, liqueurs, and brandies are named after the places where they were first made, and are, therefore, toponyms. But to qualify for this book, a word must have developed a different or additional sense than simply the source of a beverage or breed first produced there. *Chartreuse* certainly meets this test in that it is an aromatic liqueur made by the Carthusian monks at Grenoble, France. In addition, *chartreuse* in its lower-case form is also a clear light green with a yellow tinge, the color of the best *Chartreuse*.

La Grande Chartreuse, the mother home of this order, was founded by St. Bruno of Cologne in A.D.1086, according to custom. The monks did not, however, start producing the liqueur until the seventeenth century when the Marechal d'Estrees gave the monks the recipe for this famous beverage. The English word *charterhouse* is said to be an anglicized form of Carthusian, or *Chartreuse*. The *Charterhouse*, one of the leading public schools in London, England, was founded in 1611 for poor boys. It is said to have been built on the site of an old Carthusian monastery, hence its current name.

Liqueur and, for that matter, liquor are derived from the Latin word *liquere*, to drink. A liqueur is any alcoholic liquor, usually strong, sweet, and highly flavored. Such drinks are often called *cordials*, a word that is derived from the Latin *cor*, the heart, because of it's heart-warming and stimulative effect. When consumed in sufficient quantity, cordials can also render the partaker more congenial. Brandy is derived from the Dutch word *brandewyn* which means burnt (i.e., distilled) wine and is an alcoholic liquor distilled from the fermented juice of grapes or other fruits. An alcoholic beverage, therefore, could be described as a cordial, liqueur, or brandy if it was distilled from wine.

chateaubriand

Vicomte Francois Rene de Chateaubriand (1768–1848) was a minor noble who survived the turbulent years of the French Revolution. His claim to royal blood was assured by his father who sunk all of the family's small fortune in an estate at Combourg, France, complete with a medieval castle. The source of the family name is traced to an estate in Chateaubriant, a commune in the Loire Valley.

Chateaubriand had a colorful and varied political career. He was a royalist at precisely the wrong time in French history. In fact, he fought on the royalist side, was seriously wounded, but was able to escape to England where he recuperated. Prior to the revolution, he spent a short time in America where he gathered valuable experiences that he later incorporated into his literary efforts. Conditions eventually improved in France and he returned and obtained a series of diplomatic posts under Napoleon and his successors. Chateaubriand was also a man of letters and ranked highly as one of France's most important figures in Romantic literature.

His name has endured, however, mainly because of the gustatorial creativity of his chef who concocted a specialty that he named after his employer. The *chateaubriand* steak consists of a double-thick tenderloin cut of beef into which a pocket is cut and stuffed with various seasonings before grilling.

Chautauqua Circuit

How did people entertain themselves before motion pictures, television, and so on? The answer to this query would probably have been, "Very well, thank you." One very popular form of entertainment in the PVC (Pre Video and Cinema) era was provided by the **lyceums** that started in the nineteenth century. These lyceums provided adult entertainment in religion, education, music, art, and drama. The first such lyceum in the United States started in 1826.

In the summer of 1874, on the shores of Lake Chautauqua in New York State, a Methodist minister, John Vincent, along with Lewis Miller, established an assembly to promote **Bible** study in Sunday schools. It later expanded its curriculum to include a variety of subjects and in its peak year, 1924, a traveling

Chautauqua Circuit visited approximately 10,000 communities and was attended by 40 million people. By 1932, the *Chautauqua Circuit* was declining rapidly. Its slide was brought about by motion pictures, automobiles, greater sophistication, and service and lunch clubs.

Today, *Chautauqua* is a permanent resort village that still offers a full range of cultural programs each summer. The circuit has disappeared, but Chautauqua, according to William Safire, has become a generic word meaning "grass-roots intellectualism."

cheap/cheap shot/cheapskate/ cheapo

In linguistic parlance, *pejoration* is the change in a word to a less respectable meaning. *Cheap*, meaning relatively low in price, is an excellent example of a word's decline. We can trace our focal word back to the Latin word *cauponis*, a merchant. It later surfaced as *ceap*, an Old English word that meant to barter or sell well into the Shakespearean period. As the "c" in *ceap* changed from a hard "k" sound to soft "ch," it began to develop the new sense of a bargain. One major bargain center was in London, England, and was called *Cheapside*, a place where Londoners could barter with merchants and hopefully buy goods at low or *cheap* prices. It was this process of bargaining for a low price that resulted in the change in the meaning of *cheap* to the current inexpensive definition. *Cheapside* was somehow involved in the evolution of this word. Similar market centers were established in other parts of England, and versions of *cheap* were incorporated into the names of other English towns such as Chipstead, in Kent, and Chepstow, in Monmouthshire.

During *cheap's* etymological evolution, it developed several pejorative offspring. *Cheap shot*, for example, is an unsportsmanlike and illegal act of deliberate roughness, especially in football, and can also mean a malicious insult or action. The word *cheapskate* combines *cheap* with *skate*, a word with several meanings including, in this case, shit. The current sense of *cheapskate* is a person who is miserly, stingy, or simply a *cheapo*.

Cheshire cat, grin like a

In 1865, Lewis Carroll wrote *Alice's Adventures in Wonderland*, usually referred to as *Alice in Wonderland*, in which he introduced a grinning Cheshire cat that, except for its wide grin, slowly disappeared. And while Carroll is often associated with the idiom, we have evidence of a much earlier usage. Grose, for instance, listed it in his *Dictionary of the Vulgar Tongue* published in 1785. Henley's *A Dictionary of Slang* published in 1782 gives credit for its first appearance in print to a book by Wolcot entitled *A Pair of Lyric Epistles:* "Lo, like a Cheshire cat our Court will grin."

To grin like a cheshire cat is defined as laughing broadly; to laugh all over one's face; to grin so heartily as to show one's gums. The idiom generally is used to describe people who show their teeth and gums when they laugh. Some sources indicate that in the nineteenth century this expression was followed by *eating cheese, chewing gravel, or evacuating bones*.

Most authorities claim ignorance on the origin of this expression. I found one explanation, however, that intrigued me and I, therefore, offer this cheesy little tidbit to you. Cheshire cheese—a hard cheese, yellowish, orange, or white in color, made of cow's milk and similar to cheddar—was at one time sold in Cheshire (originally Chester), England, and molded like a widely grinning cat.

cheval-de-frise/ Maginot line mentality

Friesland is a chain of islands off the coast of the Netherlands and West Germany in the North Sea (see **frieze**). The Frisians are a fiercely independent Germanic people who specialize in raising cattle and, at one time, produced a rare breed of horse known by the French as *cheval-de-frise,* horse of Friesland. Early in their history (circa the fifth century) they, along with the Angles, Saxons, and Jutes, joined the great Germanic migration to Britain.

Later, in the seventeenth century, they maintained their independence with the help of the special equine breed they developed, the *cheval-de-frise,* that was not a horse at all, but a portable obstacle, usually a sawhorse, covered with spikes or barbed wire. They were used in closing a passage or creating a defensive wall. Although these military versions of the hobby horse were first used by the Frisians, they were named by the French.

The French must have been very impressed with the *cheval-de-frise,* because between 1925 and 1930 they developed their own defensive barrier based on the same idea as that of the Frisians. This line of defensive fortifications, the *Maginot line,* was named after André Maginot (1877–1932), the French Minister of War at the time. It was built along France's border with Germany, but proved to be useless when the French were outflanked in 1940 by the Germans who attacked around the *Maginot line* through Belgium.

The *Maginot line* has come to mean, idiomatically, any elaborate line of defense or set of barriers. *Maginot line mentality* is another idiom that describes actions that are defensive rather than offensive.

Chicago bankroll/ Chicago overcoat/ Chicago piano/Chicago pineapple

In the seventeenth century, something must have smelled pretty bad in the area of what is now Chicago, because the origin of this major U.S. city's name certainly suggests this. One popular interpretation has Chicago descending from *chicagou*, an Algonquin word meaning stinking, while another etymology has it coming from the Ojibwa word *she-kag-ong*, wild onion place. In the 1920s, life in Chicago once again had a bad stench when Al Capone's (1899–1947) gang ran most of the illegal operations in that city. Several interesting idioms using the Chicago name developed during this gangland era, including:

Chicago bankroll a big roll of bills, mostly ones, with a few big bills on the outside to make it look more impressive than it actually is.

Chicago overcoat a coffin.

Chicago piano a submachine gun used during World War II by the British Navy as a nickname for a rapid-fire automatic anti-aircraft gun.

Chicago pineapple a small bomb used during the prohibition era.

Chicano. See **bohunk.**

China/chinaware/bone china/ china chin/China clipper/china clipper/ China White/Chinese fire drill/ China syndrome/China hand

The Chinese invented a type of porcelain that became known as *china* as early as the Chou dynasty (1027–256 B.C.), but it wasn't perfected until the T'ang dynasty (A.D.618–907). Its Chinese origin explains why all *porcelain* (a word that is derived from the Latin word *porcus*, a pig, because of its resemblance to a pig's back) is called *china* or *chinaware*. *China* is distinguished from ordinary pottery because of its translucent quality. *Bone china* is an English development of circa 1750, and is so called because it contains a large proportion of calcium phosphate in the form of bone ash. What follows is a chop suey of slang expressions for your pleasure, including three that are derived from *chinaware*. (*Chop suey*, incidentally, comes from the Mandarin phrase *tsa sui*, meaning various things.)

china chin refers to a prize fighter who is easily knocked out when hit on the chin; also glass jaw.

China clipper a very fast ship designed in the mid-nineteenth century to reduce time on long sea voyages, particularly those involved in China trade. The *China clipper* is also lower-cased to humorously describe a dishwasher because of his or her tendency to clumsily bang dishes around during the washing process, resulting in chipping.

China the teeth (1950). "Smile and show that *china*," from the movie *Riding High*.

China White an excellent grade of heroin.

Chinese fire drill something incredibly confused.

China syndrome a nuclear accident that hypothetically results in a melt through the reactor floor and burrows into the earth until it reaches China.

China hand/China watcher a reporter, businessperson, or political observer who watches the Chinese scene to sift official statements for hidden meanings.

Chinaman's chance, he hasn't a

Today, Asians living in the United States are admired for their intelligence and work ethic. But at one stage of U.S. history, the Chinese were denied the same rights afforded to most others. Resentment against the tide of Chinese immigrants who streamed into this country during and after the California gold rush was very strong. As a result, legal barriers were raised by California and later congressional legislatures that prevented the Chinese from entering the country. These laws were not struck down until after World War II.

Asians were accustomed to working for very low wages in their homelands and were willing to work for salaries well below their **caucasian** counterparts in the United States. This fact did not endear them to other workers. In the lawless gold fields, the mining claims of the Chinese were often jumped by others, and Chinese men rarely got a fair shake in any dispute with a caucasian. This unfair treatment of the Chinese gave rise to the use of the expression, *he hasn't got a Chinaman's chance,* which means not the slightest chance; negligible odds.

Chinese solution/ Tiananmen (also Tienanmen)

Observing the creation of new words or idioms is a fascinating endeavor that can tell us much about history. Momentous historical events have resulted in the creation of many new words and phrases, some of which have lingered on for hundreds and sometimes thousands of years, often after the initial meaning of the actual episode had been lost in antiquity. A few examples from this book include **Cannae, blarney, balkanization, bunk, Bay of Pigs,** and **bikini.**

In 1989 and 1990 we witnessed unprecedented challenges to the political structure of Communist nations from eastern Europe to China. These momentous events, like many others throughout history, have produced—and continue to produce—new words and phrases. Following are two idioms that have resulted from these events.

This sentence appeared in *The New York Times* on November 19, 1989: "The turning point came on October 7, after the Communist Party leader, Erich Honecker, ordered security forces to be prepared to open fire on the demonstration in Leipzig—a '*Chinese solution*' to the rising tide of dissent in East Germany." The use of the *Chinese solution* phrase was repeated less than a month later on December 12, 1989, on the television program *Washington Week in Review*. It refers to the brutal repression of the Chinese people's demonstrations in pursuit of greater democracy; the spontaneous rallies that occurred in Tiananmen Square, Beijing, and elsewhere in June of 1989; or simply brutal repression. *Tiananmen* was also used as a synonym for repression in the same *Washington Week in Review* program mentioned above.

Within two months of the October 7 "turning point," Erich Honecker and the entire East German Politboro were either thrown out of power or resigned, and without the feared *Chinese solution*. Political changes of this magnitude rarely occur without violence. In this case, perhaps, the people of East Germany were wise enough to avoid a *Chinese solution*.

clink

As a long-time collector and classifier of word and phrase origins, I am continually amused by the interesting and sometimes charming names applied to the most unpleasant things and places. Take, for instance, the nicknames of prisons which often have such childlike names (*clink, jail, cooler, can, stir, jug, pokey, slammer, hoosegow,* and *calabooze*) that you almost want to go there. Only one of these names, *clink,* is a toponym, but I shall exercise my literary license and provide the origins of all of them. (*Note:* This author has never obtained his literary license, and hopefully will not end up in the *clink* as a result.)

A Glossary of Prison Nicknames

clink was actually the name of a prison in the Southwark district of London that can be traced at least as far back as 1550. A *clink* is defined as a prison; jail; lockup.

jail can be traced to a Latin word meaning cage, a fact that explains the use of the term *jail bird*. In England, *jail* is spelled *gaol,* but both are pronounced the same.

pen is an elliptical (shortened) version of *penitentiary* where criminals do penance for their crimes.

cooler/can have unknown origins. They first appeared in print in 1884 and 1916, respectively. We can speculate that the *cooler* cooled off the criminal while the can confined and prevented him or her from committing other crimes.

stir is derived from the gypsy (Romany) word *staripan*, meaning prison.

jug originally came from the Scandinavian and French word *joug*, an iron yoke or pillory that enclosed the hands and head. When the *joug*, anglicized to *yoke*, was abolished and replaced by jails, the word *joug* or *jug* was transferred to the jails.

pokey according to the late John Ciardi, is derived from the French word *poche*, a pocket or small enclosure. It was later anglicized to *pokey*.

slammer is echoic (a word that imitates sound) and, in this case, is imitative of the sound of the prison gate slamming shut on a convicted person.

hoosegow is derived from the Spanish word *juzgado*, a courtroom, where a prisoner is judged before being freed or confined.

calaboose is an American English version of the Spanish word *calabozo*, dungeon.

Clydesdale

Many names of horses, dogs, and cats are toponymous, and while their places of origin are interesting, only a few unusual varieties are included in this book.

The heaviest horses are called *draft* (or draw) horses, a word that is derived from the Old English word *dragen*, to pull or draw. The animal considered to be the handsomest of this class is the *Clydesdale,* a breed from Lanarkshire, Scotland, where the Clyde River flows. The average size of the *Clydesdale* is 16 to 16 and one-half hands, and the average weight is approximately 1,700 pounds.

The *Clydesdale* has two unique features that distinguish it from other breeds. First, it has long flowing hair or "feather" below the knee, and second, it is usually seen as part of a team pulling an Anheuser-Busch beer wagon. I am curious to know if the Anheuser-Busch Company will be using smaller horses in the future to pull wagons full of their light beer. Incidentally, the second element in Clydesdale, *dale,* means valley.

coach

The word *coach,* as in the horse-drawn *coach,* the *coach* class aboard airlines, and the educational or athletic *coach,* all come from the same place, *Kocs,* a small town in northwest Hungary near Budapest. It was in this town that the first horse-drawn *coach* was invented in the fifteenth century. The use of these large passenger vehicles quickly spread throughout Europe, because they provided cheap transportation for the commoners who could not afford their own conveyances.

The spelling of this placename and carriage varied as its popularity spread throughout Europe. For example, the Spanish and Portuguese version was *coche;* Italian, *cocchio;* Dutch, *koets;* Polish, *kocz.* By the eighteenth century, *Kocs* was anglicized to *coach.* A century later the word *coach* was synonymous with English university tutors, apparently because they, too, carried their students along, albeit educationally. By the late nineteenth century, *coach* was also used as the name for one who trained or managed athletic teams.

The word *coach* went airborne in the twentieth century as the airline industry elected to designate the second-class passenger section of a plane as the *coach* class. This word has taken a long and varied journey, via carriage class, from the harsh roads of Hungary in the fifteenth century, to the "friendly skies" of the twentieth century.

coffee/mocha

Coffee's credentials as a toponym rely heavily on a legend that places its initial discovery in the town of Kaffa in southwestern Ethiopia. This stimulating theory is further advanced by the *Encyclopedia Britannica,* which suggests that the discovery of *coffee's* innervating effect can be traced to Kaldi, a goatherd from Kaffa. Kaldi, according to this legend, was the first to notice his goats' unusual capers (*caper* is the Latin word for goat) after eating the beans of the Kaffa plant.

Kaldi apparently ate the beans himself and he too enjoyed their effect. So it is no wonder that man's first use of the coffee bean was as a food or medicine. Later, coffee was used to make a wine and finally a nonalcoholic beverage. *Coffee* reached Arabia in the thirteenth century where the Arabic word for the plant and its byproducts was *qahwah* (probably an *Arabesque* version of Kaffa). As coffee's popularity traveled westward to Turkey, Italy, and France, *qahwah* became *café* and finally *coffee.*

One very choice variety of coffee, *mocha,* is also derived from a placename, the Arab seaport of Mukha in what is now southern Yemen. It was from this port that *mocha* was first exported. Today, this versatile word is also used to describe a mixture of chocolate and *coffee,* as well as a brownish chocolate color.

cologne

In the year A.D. 50, a city was founded by the Romans on a bend in the Rhine River. According to legend and historical accounts, this city was named Colonnia Agrippina (Agrippina's Colony) because it was the birthplace of Agrippina, the wife of the reigning Roman Emperor, Claudius. The name of the city was later shortened to Colonnia. And while the German word for the city is now *Koln,* during its French occupation it was called *Cologne.* We are starting to pick up the scent of *cologne,* a scented water produced there since 1709. Perfume, though, was first developed in the Orient and brought to Europe by the Crusaders around 1200.

Despite the fact that the word *cologne* is now loosely used to mean scented water or toilet water, within the perfume industry such terms are more precise. For instance:

perfume consists of 10 to 20 percent perfume oils dissolved in alcohol.

cologne contains 3 to 5 percent perfume oils dissolved in 80 to 90 percent alcohol with water making up the balance.

toilet water contains 2 percent perfume oils in 60 to 80 percent alcohol, and the balance is water.

Scents for men have become widely accepted and the industry has adapted the word *cologne* for such manly odors. Perhaps a *cologne* by any other name just wouldn't *sell* as sweetly.

colophon

There are Colophonians on the U.S. East Coast (Colophon, New Jersey), and there are Californians on the U.S. West Coast, but there are no longer any Colophonians in Colophon (Kolophon), Turkey. Kolophon was an ancient city, one of the 12 Ionian cities in Asia Minor, which was depopulated in 286 B.C. (Incidentally, California is not in any way related to Colophon. *California* was a Spanish shaping of *Califerne,* an imaginary land, which first appeared in the epic poem, Chanson de Roland, about the battle of Roncevaux Pass [see **runcible spoon**].) Colophonia here we come.

Ancient Kolophon was noted for its legendary cavalry which was such a superb fighting force that any side on which it fought was assured of victory. The word eventually entered the English language as *colophon,* the finishing touch. *Colophon* is currently defined as an inscription usually placed at the end of a book giving information pertaining to its publication. It is also a publisher's emblem or trademark placed on the title page or binding.

Conestoga wagons. See **stogie.**

Coney Island

At the southwestern end of Long Island lies *Coney Island,* a beach and amusement park that is a part of the New York City borough of Brooklyn. It is, however, an island in name only, since landfill now connects it with Brooklyn.

The early Dutch settlers named this amusing place *Kunyen Eyland,* meaning rabbit island, because of the large hare population that at one time resided there. Today, *Coney Island* is better known for a quite different animal, the hot dog.

In some regions of the United States, hot dogs are known as *Coney Islands,* because of the many hot dog stands that could be found there. The most famous of those food concessions is Nathan's, which is now a chain serving hot dogs as well as other fast foods. *Coney Island gold,* a nickname for mustard, was also inspired by the "Island's" association with the hot dog.

copper

About 10,000 years ago, prehistoric man discovered a reddish metal that could be hammered into a variety of utensils, weapons, and ornaments. Five thousand years later, large deposits of this *copper* metal were discovered on the island of Cyprus. This island subsequently became a battleground for a succession of ancient powers bent on controlling this essential element—powers including the Egyptians, Assyrians, Phoenicians, Greeks, Persians, and Romans.

The metal was known by the Romans as *aes cyprium*, "ore of Cyprus." *Cyprium* evolved into *cyprum*, which eventually entered the English language as *copper*. The value of *copper* ore was heightened by the discovery that when mixed with tin it became bronze (during the Bronze Age, circa 3000 B.C.); and when alloyed with zinc it produced brass.

Copper is also a slang word for police. The notion that this was due to the use of *copper* buttons on police uniforms is a true example of false etymology. The metallic nickname for law officers does not come from the metal, but rather from the Latin word *capere*, to capture or nab.

Corinthian/currant

Archaeologists claim that, at one time, ancient Corinth had a population of over one million, mostly fun-loving, citizens. Corinth's reputation for wickedness was so great, in fact, that it inspired Saint Paul, a disciple of Jesus, to minister to its citizens in A.D. 54 and write Corinthians I and II (the seventh and eighth books of the New Testament). The importance of this Greek city-state resulted, for the most part, from its location on the isthmus that connects the Peloponnesus with the rest of Europe. American archaeologists did not begin their initial excavations at Corinth until 1896.

The *Corinthian* column is one of the three Greek architectural orders. It is considerably more decorative than the other two (Doric and Ionic). The *Corinthian* column is distinguished by a bell-shaped cone surrounded by two rows of acanthus leaves and pairs of branching scrolls at its four corners. This special architectural embellishment was said to have been inspired by a basket of acanthus leaves which the order's creator happened upon one day in the marketplace.

Corinth is also remembered for the *Corinth* grapes and raisins that they exported and which was anglicized to *currant*. Of somewhat lesser currency is the use of *Corinthian* to describe a man about town. This use developed around the proverbially lewd activities of the *Corinthians* of old.

Coventry, send to/ Coventry blue

A person could be *sent to Coventry* but never actually get there. For, you see, this idiom has come to mean a state of ostracism, in which one is openly and pointedly ignored. How did this city in the West Midlands of England come to be used in this idiomatic way? There are several explanations, but the following one seems best attested and most plausible.

According to Brewer, the people of *Coventry* had an inordinate hatred of soldiers. So strong was this attitude that they would not so much as talk to a soldier. Even young women were ostracized if they were seen talking to a member of the military. As you might imagine, *Coventry* was not a favorite place for a soldier to spend a tour of duty. In fact, it was considered the worst possible place to be assigned.

There is also a *Coventry blue,* which was a color-fast dye made in Coventry. It represented a vast improvement over other available dyes that were not as fast. This special dye of Coventry is a possible source of the expression *true blue,* used to describe a person of unswerving loyalty—probably because such a person will not run when you most need him or her.

cravat

The necktie has been making a fashion statement for thousands of years, and in at least two instances has been popularized by the military. *Focale,* for instance, was the name for a neck kerchief worn by ancient Roman soldiers. In 1660, a regiment of mercenaries from Croatia visited Paris, France. Croatia is now a region of northern Yugoslavia bounded by the Adriatic Sea. On that auspicious occasion in the seventeenth century, the Croatians, whom the French called *Cravate,* were in the pay of the Austrians. The Croatian parade regalia included brightly colored handkerchiefs worn around the neck. This bit of flair was greatly admired by the always fashion-minded French, and the wearing of *cravates* or *cravats* quickly became a fad, but one that remains with us to this day.

Cretan/cretin/cretonne/ creticism

Cretan is a legitimate toponym, while *cretin* is not. But since the two are often confused, it's worth some clarification. *Cretonne* is also a genuine toponym.

A *Cretan* is a native of Crete, but the word would not have qualified for inclusion in this toposaurus on that distinction alone. Crete, an island in the eastern Mediterranean, is 160 miles long and 6 to 35 miles wide. It is the site of the ancient palace of Knossos. *Cretans* had a reputation as liars and the word *cretan* survives, though it is somewhat obscure in this sense. *Cretin,* on the other hand, is a more commonly used word, and is a shortened version of the Old French word *Chrestian,* a Christian. *Cretin* was first used to describe a colony of congenitally deformed idiots living in the Swiss Alps. It later developed its current derogatory meaning as someone who is stupid or obtuse.

Cretonne is another instance in which a special fabric was named for its place of origin, Creton, a village in Normandy, France. *Cretonne* is a cotton, linen, or rayon material in colorfully printed designs, used especially for draperies or slip covers.

Finally, if you have any *creticism* (sic) for the author's decision to combine these four words in one essay, I wouldn't blame you. The *Oxford English Dictionary* defines *creticism* as the act of lying.

Curaçao

Curaçao is the largest island in the Netherlands Antilles in the Caribbean Sea, 60 miles north of northwest Venezuela. This small island, 30 miles long by 8 miles wide, was discovered by the Spaniards in 1449 and was settled in 1527. The Dutch West India Company captured Curaçao in 1634. Etymologist Adrian Room provides us with an explanation for the origin of Curaçao, and despite the fact that I have been unable to corroborate it, it is nevertheless worthy of note here.

Room claims that the Spaniards, after their first visit to this island which was originally named *Isla de los Gigantes* (Island of the Giants), left behind several allegedly terminally ill soldiers. A few years later, the Spaniards returned and found the same soldiers completely cured and living among the natives. As a result of this medical miracle, according to Room, they renamed the island *Curacion,* a Spanish word meaning cure.

A liqueur known generically as *curaçao* was originally produced on the island but was later modified and made in Europe. Today's *curaçaos* consist of distilled alcohol infused with bitter orange peels grown on Curaçao, as well as syrup, brandies, rum, ethereal oils, and spices. The liqueur is marketed under a number of labels including Grand Marnier and Triple Sec. *Curaçao* by any other of its names will probably taste as sweet, but it will not cure anything except perhaps, sobriety.

currant. See **Corinthian.**

DDDDDDDDDDD**D**DDDDDDDDDDD

damask/Damascus steel/damascene/ damson plum

Damascus is an ancient city in, and the capital of, Syria. It is reputed to be the oldest continuously existing city in the world and currently has a population of over 1.2 million. Damascus was ruled by the Egyptians and Hittites before it became an independent kingdom around 1000 B.C. This eternal city needs no help from its toponyms to keep its name alive. And yet, this *damascene* word loom has exported many items bearing its name, a fact that tends to keep it immortal. (*Damascene* indicates something similar to Damascus or its products.)

Damask is a reversible fabric of linen, silk, cotton, or wool with patterns woven in. It is currently produced in a variety of places around the world, but gets its name from the fact that it was originally manufactured in Damascus. This ageless Middle Eastern city is also known for its *Damascus steel,* a hand-wrought steel, made in various Asian countries from metal sheets, repeatedly folded over, welded, and finally etched to reveal the resulting grain; these were used for sword blades. The final plum from this *damascene* source is the *damson plum,* a variety of small purple plum that grows on a rose tree. *Damson* is an alteration of *damascene.*

Dan to Beersheba, from

The ancient world of the **Bible** was truly a microcosm (a world in miniature). This can be illustrated by a phrase from the Old Testament (Judges 20:1) "from Dan to Beersheba." This expression was later popularized by the literary world, and it came to mean from one extreme place to another; all over the known world. The distance between *Dan and Beersheba,* though a mere 150 miles, was considered at one time to encompass the whole world. The northern pole of this tiny world was *Dan,* an ancient village at the northern extreme of Palestine currently on Israel's border with Lebanon, but today merely a mound.

Beersheba, on the other hand, is a town in southern Israel (about 45 miles south of Jerusalem) with a population today of over 100,000 people. Several other placenames come to mind that are used idiomatically to express humankind's concept of a faraway place or simply the limits of our world. They include:

Thule, ultima the furthest point; the limit of any journey. This imaginary place comes from a Latin phrase which represented the land furthest north—at least as far as the ancient Romans knew.

Timbuktu, from here to from here to any very faraway place. Timbuktu (French Tombouctou) is a town in Central Mali, West Africa, near the Niger River. It remains an important trade center on the Sahara Camel caravan routes.

The outer limits of the modern world are measured in light-years (the distance traversed by light in one mean solar year, about 5.88 trillion miles.) *Light-years* has come to mean a very great distance, especially in development or progress. The world has progressed light-years from *Dan* to *Beersheba.*

Dead Sea fruit

Have you ever looked upon something that looked very good, but upon closer inspection or use turned out to be a big disappointment? The object of such an experience is occasionally called *Dead Sea fruit*. Thus begins our salty story.

The Dead Sea is a salt lake located between Israel and Jordan. It is approximately 46 miles long, 10 miles wide, and roughly 1,300 feet below sea level, making it the lowest lake in the world. The salt content of this lake is over 26 percent compared to the oceans which have a 3 to 4 percent salt content. It is reported that orange and apple trees grow on the shores of this lake. The fruit of such trees is reputed to look very nice but actually tastes terrible because of its high content of salt and other minerals. Its bad taste is the basis for the expression *Dead Sea fruit* which aptly describes something that appears to be beautiful or full of promise but is actually nothing but illusion and disappointment. This is the kind of experience that can leave a bad taste in your mouth.

Delphi/Delphic Oracle

Delphi was a seventh-century B.C. Greek religious center situated between Mt. Parnassus and the Gulf of Corinth. Like Olympia (see **Olympic Games**), it was the site of quadrennial athletic contests known as the Pythian games. It was also renowned for its Temple of Apollo and, of course, the *Delphic Oracle* that resided there.

Delphi, a word that is thought to come from the Greek *delphoi*, meaning brothers, is a reference to the twin peaks of Mt. Parnassus that loomed high above this religious/sports/arts center. In Greek mythology, *Delphi* was considered to be the navel of the earth. It was at the exact site of this navel that the Temple of Apollo was built, from which the *Delphic oracles* were said to give forth their oracular pronouncements.

Although the oracles' pronouncements were usually obscure or ambiguous, pilgrims from around the Greek world traveled there to be enlightened (or confused). *Delphi's* importance in the ancient world is attested to by its continued idiomatic use in modern English in the adjective *Delphic,* which has come to mean obscure in meaning or ambiguous.

denims. See **jeans.**

Derby/derby

Tucked away in the Midlands of England is the county borough of Derby, the capital of Derbyshire county and the home of Epsom Downs race track. It was there that the original *Derby,* named after and instituted by Edward Stanley, twelfth Earl of Derby, was run in 1780. This *Derby* also gave its name to other important horse-racing events, including the Kentucky Derby classic for three-year-olds run at Churchill Downs on the first Saturday in May every year since 1875. To top things off, this toponym was also used as the name of a hat, the *derby* (also called a bowler), a stiff hat with rounded crown and narrow brim worn at the Derby and named after the Earl who instituted it.

The word *derby* can also be used to denote any endeavor regarded as competition; *to win the gubernatorial derby,* for instance. *Derby* combines the Old English (Anglo-Saxon) word *deor,* meaning deer, and the Scandinavian place suffix, *-by,* meaning village; literally a deer village or park. The *derby* hat may be a thing of the past, but the Derby races have certainly remained popular.

dollar

We searched high and low, over hill and through deserts, but finally found the origin of *dollar,* the worldwide standard of value, in a *dale* or valley. For the story of this word we must take you back to the sixteenth century to a region in Bohemia (see **bohemian**) known as *Joachimsthal,* literally St. Joseph's Valley. *Thal* is a placename suffix that means valley.

It was in that valley in 1519 that the Counts of Schlick resided and minted coins that came from the family's own silver mine. These coins were known as *Joachimsthalers,* which local people shortened to *thalers.* When these *thalers* reached the land of the Dutch, the word *thaler* was altered to *daler,* which the English rounded out to *dollar.*

The phrase "almighty dollar" was coined by Washington Irving in 1836. Incidentally, Joachimsthal is now in Czechoslovakia. Any coins minted there today could well glow in the dark, because they now mine uranium and not silver in the town now called *Jachymov.*

donnybrook

There's a wee place with the sweet-sounding name of *Donnybrook,* which is adjacent to and southeast of Dublin, Ireland. The early meaning of *Donnybrook* was simply town marsh, and I suspect that *Donnybrook* was originally just a poor stretch of bottom land near Ireland's biggest city. *Donnybrook* has traveled far, however, to develop its lower-case meaning of a brawl, uproar, or free-for-all.

Etymologists have had a field day, if not a *donnybrook,* on the story surrounding this idiom. Ernest Weekley, for example, believes that there were wild bacchanalian and saturnalian festivals held there in pagan days, while John Ciardi pinpoints A.D. 1204 as the year when *Donnybrook* was granted permission to hold an annual two-week fair. All agree, however, that these annual fairs frequently got out of hand and were often the site of drunken brawls. It got so bad, in fact, that the fair was officially suppressed in 1855, but its namesake, *donnybrook,* is still alive and now synonymous with the brawls, contentious disputes, or free-for-alls that occur anywhere.

duffel/duffel bag

Every person who ever went to camp or who served in the U.S. military has gotten well acquainted with the *duffel bag,* a cylindrical bag used for carrying personal belongings. The *duffel bag* is an American invention despite the fact that the word *duffel* is derived from Duffel, a town of Brabant (a former duchy in western Europe, now divided between Belgium and the Netherlands) near Antwerp where it was first produced. *Duffel* was a coarse woolen cloth having a thick nap or **frieze** that has long been used for blankets and coats. In fact, the *Oxford English Dictionary* notes that "*duffel* coats" were given to the Minisink Indians (American) in 1684.

Other toponymous fabrics similar to *duffel* include *kersey,* especially made for work clothes in Kersey, Suffolk, England. *Melton* is another duffel-like fabric which was first woven in Melton, Mowbray, England; it is a heavy cloth, often of wool, tightly constructed and finished with a smooth face concealing the weave. It is used for coats, hunting jackets, and the like.

The *duffel* is in no way connected with *duff,* a word that is synonymous with the buttocks. Anyone with experience in the military, however, can tell you that during many long waits while in transit, one's *duff* was often connected to one's *duffel* for "endless" periods of time.

dumdum

A *dumdum* (unhyphenated) is a hollow-nosed or soft-nosed bullet that expands on impact, inflicting a severe wound; it is also called a *dumdum bullet.* The name of this deadly projectile is derived from Dum-Dum (hyphenated), a district of West Bengal, India (7 miles northeast of Calcutta). There are actually three Dum-Dums; North Dum-Dum, South Dum-Dum, and just plain Dum-Dum, which was the headquarters of the Bengal artillery until 1853. This facility had an ammunition factory where the *dumdum bullet* was first manufactured in the late 1890s.

dungarees. See jeans.

Dunkirk/Dunkirk, to do a

Young people today use the verb to *book* meaning to leave a place quickly. While I have not found an explanation for this slang idiom as yet, I believe it may be a shortened version of the English expression *to book passage* as on a steamship, train, or plane. The origin of *to do a Dunkirk,* meaning to evacuate a place, is more easily traced. It is a reference to the miraculous evacuation of the British Expeditionary Force and its allies from the tiny port of Dunkirk, France, in 1940. This army, totaling 330,000 men, quickly left France between May 29 and June 4, 1940. Winston Churchill called this evacuation, "a miracle of deliverance." Their hasty retreat was made necessary after the Belgians had laid down their arms in World War II, making the position of the Brits and their allies untenable. *Dunkirk* has also come to mean a period of crisis or emergency during which drastic measures must be enforced.

Dunkirk is a port town in northeast France on the North Sea. The town grew up around the church of St. Eloi, and the name of the town was derived from the Flemish words *duine,* meaning dune, and *kirk,* church, or literally church on the dune. The evacuation was carried out by thousands of small craft including English pleasure craft, many of which had never previously left the Thames.

Dutch

The following explains why the Netherlands is also known as Holland, while its people are known as the *Dutch*. In addition, it explains the reason for the many uncomplimentary idioms involving the *Dutch* word.

Three hundred years ago, the people of this low country on the west coast of northern Europe called themselves *Diets*, the people. This word was applied to all German people and it was later anglicized to *Dutch*. The *Netherlands*, on the other hand, combines *Nether-*, below, and *-land*, and describes the lowlands at the mouth of the Rhine River also known as the low countries. The name Holland is also applied to this country. But Holland was simply a province of the Netherlands that eventually became synonymous with the whole country.

During the seventeenth century, the English and the *Dutch* were competitors in international commerce. As a result of this rivalry, the English developed several uncomplimentary idioms involving the *Dutch* name:

Dutch treat a dinner at which each guest pays his or her own way.

Dutch auction one that starts with a high bid and descends until someone accepts a lower offer. This is the exact opposite of how most auctions are conducted.

Dutch courage courage acquired from drinking alcoholic beverages.

Dutchman a word often used in the construction industry to describe something that is done to hide poor work.

Dutch reckoning guesswork.

Dutch, in in disgrace; in trouble or disfavor.

Dutch bargain a purchase that turns out to be more expensive than it should be.

Dutch defense surrender or retreat.

Dutch uncle a stern or critical adviser.

The relationship between the Dutch and English is very good today, but the pejorative *Dutch* idioms have survived. Such is the nature of idioms. Their usefulness often outlives their original intended sense.

EEEEEEEEEEEEEEEEEEEEEEEEE

Elysian/Elysian fields/ Champs Elysees

Many ancient pagan religions had their own heaven and hell, as do our more modern theologies. For example, in the classical Greek mythology, Elysium was the abode of the blessed dead. *Elysium* is elliptical (a shortened version) for the older phrase *Elysium pedion*, which translates into English as *Elysian fields*. *Elysium* was in effect the Greek equivalent of heaven, paradise, or **Valhalla.** *Elysian* is currently defined as happy, delightful, or blissful. Spencer used *Elysian fields* in *The Shepard's Pie* (1579), while Shakespeare included it in *Two Gentlemen of Verona* (1594–1595).

The Latin version of *Elysium pedion* was *elysii compi*, which translates into modern French as *Champs Elysees*, the name of a Parisian shopping avenue, once one of the finest in the world (although now dominated by fast-food restaurants and movie houses). *Elysees* is also the name of a palace in Paris, which is now the official residence of the president of France. It must have been a delightful place to be so named.

English/Anglican/British/ Albion/blighty

It is incorrect to refer to the British Isles, in the period prior to A.D. 457, as England. In that year a Germanic tribe known as the Angles arrived there. The Angles eventually became dominant over the Saxons, Jutes, Frisians, aboriginal Celts, and other tribes. By A.D. 1000 the land was known as England, the land of the Engles (*Engle* was a later form of *Angle*). The people became *Anglican*, kin of the Engles, and their language became known as *Englisc*, the adjectival form of *Engle*.

Britain, a much older word for England, has several origins. Aristotle (384–322 B.C.) referred to the island as Britannic, a word thought to be derived from the Welsh word *Priten* meaning warriors. Others, including Brewer, claim that *Britain* is derived from an older Phoenician word, *Baratanic*, meaning country of tin. And, indeed, it was from Britain (England had not been invented yet) that the ancient Greeks and Romans obtained tin, a metal that is essential in the making of bronze.

England, or Britain, has two nicknames that I feel obliged to toss into this English stew. *Albion*, for example, is often used as a sobriquet for England in British literature. The Morrises suspect that *Albion* is derived from the Latin word *alba*, meaning white, and was probably a reference to the English White Cliffs of Dover.

England is affectionately referred to by the English as *old or auld blighty* as well. In this instance, *blighty* can be traced to the Hindi word *bilayati*, the country. It was borrowed and anglicized by the English, along with many other Indian words, during their long occupation of India.

English is based upon the Germanic language of the Angles. It has a predominance of Latin words provided by the Roman and French conquerors. *English* has virtually no Brythonic (Welsh) or Celtic words, however. The etymologies of Britain and England explain why the language in which this book is written is called English, and not British.

Epsom salts (also salt)/ dose of salts

Like the **derby** that also runs annually at Epsom, England, *Epsom salts* have caused some "runs" in their time, because these special *salts* are chiefly used as a cathartic (laxative, purgative). *Epsom salts* are also used in fertilizers, the dying of fabrics, and leather tanning, and were so named because they were first discovered near Epsom, England, around 1760–1770. The salts were originally obtained by boiling down the mineral water in the vicinity of Epsom but are now chemically produced. The chemical so effective in moving things right along is known as sulphate of magnesia.

Epsom and its salts figure in two other idioms. In cockney rhyming slang, for example, *Epsom races* is synonymous with, and means, "a pair of braces." *Epsom salt,* a one-time favorite in every mother's arsenal of constipation remedies, is also responsible for the expression, *a dose of salts;* this expression refers to something done quite easily or quickly.

FFFFFFFFFFFFF F FFFFFFFFFFFFF

Finlandization. See **balkanization.**

flamenco/flamingo

Spain is the birthplace of a distinctive style of dancing, *flamenco*, that is characteristic of the Andalusian Gypsies (see **gyp**). The dance is very rhythmic and combines vigorous stamping of the heels, hand clapping, and castanet clicking. While *flamenco* is of Spanish origin, it is actually a reference to the Flemish people of Flanders. Flanders is now a part of the coastal lowlands of Belgium and the French province of Nord. In Medieval times, the Flemish people were known for their ruddy complexions and bright costumes. It was in this sense that the Spanish coined the *flamenco* name for the colorful dancing of this Andalusian group.

The name of the aquatic bird *flamingo* was also inspired by the Flemings. Aside from their colorful nature, though, the *flamingo* bird and *flamenco* dance have no other connection. In the early days of television, *flamenco* dancing was a popular feature of the big variety shows such as "The Ed Sullivan Show." The dance apparently clicked with the fans of that era.

Fleet Street

The clustering in one street or area of a number of competitors in a single industry or activity has resulted in quite a few toponyms. For instance, **Madison Avenue** in New York City was at one time the address of so many advertising agencies that it eventually became synonymous (or toponymous) with the entire U.S. ad industry. Other examples are **Wall Street,** a synonym for the U.S. financial industry; Greenwich Village, for the art community; and **Grubstreet,** London, England, for **hackney** writers.

London, England, is also the location of another street, *Fleet Street,* which has become synonymous with the British newspaper world. Its name, *Fleet,* can be traced back to Medieval times when it was spelled *Flete* after a nearby stream. The origin of *Fleet* or *Flete* is the Old English word *fleot* meaning flowing water. Farmer and Henley's *A Dictionary of Slang,* first published in 1890, described *Fleet-Streetese* thusly: "The so-called English, written to sell by the Fleet Streeter, or baser sort of journalist: a mixture of sesquipedalians and slang, of phrases worn threadbare and phrases sprung from the kennel of bad grammar and worse manners. . . ." This description could be applied to some of the British press today, one hundred years after Farmer and Henley's definition. The *Fleet Street* press is also noted for its *Fleet*ness of foot in going after sensational stories to attract and titillate its readers. Today, there is not a single newspaper left on Fleet Street.

forensic

The Roman forum was, at one time, a swampy region between the Palatine (see **palace**) and Capitoline (see **capitol**) Hills. It was drained by the Etruscans in the sixth century B.C. and eventually became the heart of Rome. It served as the administrative, legislative, and legal center of the Roman Empire. There were, to be sure, many forums throughout the empire, but the Forum Romanum was the core of that ancient world. It was also a busy marketplace and was even closed to traffic like the malls (see **pell mell**) of today.

The word *forum* is taken directly from Latin, in which it is defined as a marketplace (out of doors). The Latin adjective of *forum* is *forensis* meaning situated on the outside, in this case the forum. *Forensis* was adopted and reshaped by the English language to create our focus word, *forensic*, which means pertaining to or employed in legal proceedings or argumentation, such as those that might have taken place in the Roman Forum. While *forensic* is used in connection with anthropology, chemistry, and psychiatry, it is most frequently associated with medicine. *Forensic* medicine is defined as the application of medical knowledge to questions of civil and criminal law, especially in court proceedings. *Forum* is also akin to the Latin word *foris* from which *forest* and *foreign* are derived.

franca, lingua/lingo

The tongue's importance to a spoken language is confirmed by the fact that the word *language* itself was derived from the Latin word *lingua*, meaning tongue. *Lingo* is a shortened version of *lingua franca* and is defined as the jargon or slang of a particular group or individual, for example, gambler's *lingo*. The Franks, from which *franca* was derived, were a Germanic tribe in the sixth century A.D. that ruled much of Europe and controlled trade in the Mediterranean. Originally, *lingua franca* was a mixture of Italian, Spanish, French, Greek, and Turkish languages spoken especially in the Levant (Middle East). It was a language of commerce that enabled people of diverse tongues—especially the Arabs and the western Europeans—to communicate.

Pidgin English was a later form of *lingua franca* used by British traders with China in the seventeenth century. Pidgin English was essentially a mixture of English and Chinese. The word *pidgin* developed from the Chinese pronunciation of the English word *business*. Today, there are many *lingua francas* used around the world that developed when people of differing languages suddenly came together and found it necessary to communicate. This process has been responsible for entire languages, such as French and Spanish, which are said to have developed from the linguistic collision between one of the ancient European tribes and the vulgar Latin of their Roman conquerors. The new languages resulting from these clashes are fittingly called **Romance** languages.

frank

As is the case with many other words, the word *frank,* meaning to be direct and straightforward in speech; sincere; and also free, was adapted from the name of a people, the *Franks.* (Compare **turkey, welsh,** and **slave.**) Here is my *frank* explanation of how this came about.

The word *frank* came from the Old Saxon (a German tribe) word *franko* meaning spear. Incidentally, the name *Saxon* came from their word *sahs,* or swords. The people of this region, the *Franks,* were known to be adept with the spear. When the *Franks* originally conquered the land they called *France,* they were the only free men or nobles in the land, and *franc* then came to mean free in the French language.

It was from this free sense that we get *franked mail,* the free use of postal services enjoyed by members of Congress to this day. Several proper names also came from this frank source, such as, *Franklin, Francis* (or *Frances*), and *Frankfurt,* the name of a city founded by the *Franks.* This city, which is now German, was established by the Franks on a ford (port). It was from this city that we get the **frankfurter,** a sausage.

frankfurter/weiner/hot dog

I have prepared a **frank** analysis of the origins of the *frankfurter,* a small cooked and smoked sausage of beef or pork with or without casing, and its synonyms *weiner* and *hot dog*. I hope that these tasty morsels are to your liking.

The *frankfurter,* like the **hamburger,** originally came from an ancient German city, in this case Frankfurt. According to Ernest Gill, who authored a *New York Times* article on the subject, *frankfurter* was the name given to these sausages by the people of Vienna, Austria. The people of Frankfurt, on the other hand, call these same sausages *wieners,* the name that the Viennese use to describe themselves.

The introduction of the *hot dog* idiom and fast-food favorite in the United States is attributed to Harry M. Stevens, a concessionaire at the Polo Grounds (the former home of the New York Giants baseball and football teams). Stevens advertised them as hot dachshund sausages because of their similarity to the very low-slung, short-legged, and elongated German dachshund canine breed. The hot dachshund was eventually shortened to *hot dachs,* and finally to *hot dog*(s). Stevens served them in a roll with relish and mustard. Newspaper cartoonist Tad Dorgan helped to popularize the *hot dog* in 1896 by sketching a dachshund dog in a roll, and the *hot dog* was on a roll. It became so popular, in fact, that the hot dog was and is used to mean superior or good. By 1960 the *hot dog* took a new twist adding the new sense of a show-off. It is not clear how the *hot dog* developed its show-off nuance, but it is relished by this etymologist nonetheless.

French leave/French disease, gout, pox/ French postcards, prints, novels/ pardon my French/French kiss

International rivalry and ethnic diversity often result in a volley of uncomplimentary slurs launched between the people of competing nations. This phenomenon was covered in the discussion on the word **Dutch,** as well as in the discussion on the **Punic faith,** and others. I am indebted to Hugh Rawson's fine book, *A Dictionary of Euphemisms & Other Doubletalk,* for much of the ensuing information.

French leave This idiom is defined as leaving a party without saying goodnight to the hostess. It can also be applied to a soldier who is AWOL (*A*bsent *W*ithout *O*fficial *L*eave). That this euphemism is applied to the socially proper French can only be attributed to international name-calling, as it seems to have no grounding in reality.

French disease, French gout, and French pox Each of these idioms is a satirical euphemism for syphilis. Other countries also ascribe the origin of this disease to their arch rivals. The exact source of this disease is unknown, but Rawson suggests that it was brought back from the New World by the crews of Christopher Columbus. This disease is variously known as the Neopolitan disease, the Italian disease, the Spanish disease, and so on. The name applied to the disease often depends on the nationality of the speaker.

French postcards, French prints, and French novels To the English and Americans, the word *French* is often associated with something sexy or profane. These idioms thus pertain to pictures or literature that are indelicate or racy.

French, pardon my The *French* word in this case refers to swear words and foul language in general.

French kiss A *French kiss* is an open-mouthed kiss in which the tongue comes into play.

Many of the *French* euphemistic slurs were picked up by the more puritanical American soldiers during World War I and brought back with them to enliven our tongue.

frieze

Friesland consists of a chain of isles three to twenty miles off the mainland of western Europe in the North Sea. Phrygia was an ancient country in west central Asia Minor (Turkey). Although these two lands are widely separated, they are linked etymologically, according to excellent authorities, because both lands have contributed *frieze* homonyms (words that have the same sound and in this case the same spelling).

The first *frieze* I shall discuss is the architectural term for a horizontal part of a classical entablature that rests on the columns and is immediately above the architrave and below the cornice. It also has come to mean any decorative band on an exterior wall that bears lettering or sculpture. *Frieze,* in this case, comes from Phrygia, a region of the ancient Greek world. It has been suggested that this decorative building element was inspired by the Phrygian garments that had an embroidered band of gold.

The second *frieze* is a very coarse, shaggy, woolen cloth with an uncut nap that probably came from Friesland.

Neither of these *friezes* have any etymological relationship with the word *freeze. Freeze* is another homonym of *frieze,* but this frigid form has a different spelling and is derived from an altogether different verb.

GGGGGGGGG**G**GGGGGGGGG

gallery. See mall.

See mall.

galosh (also galoshes and golosh)

A *galosh* is a waterproof overshoe, especially a high one. When I was a child, the important thing about the *galosh* was not how you spelled it (and today you still have a choice of spellings), but rather that you followed your mother's advice and wore two of them during a wet or snowy spell. And, of course, if you failed to wear them you were in for a spell of sickness which always spelled trouble from Mom.

The *galosh* was not always the water-repellent, flexible boot that we now know. The original idea for the *galosh,* and its name, can be traced back to an item of footwear attributed to the Gauls. Gaul was an ancient region in western Europe that included the modern areas of North Italy, France, Belgium, and southern Netherlands. Most reputable sources agree that the *galosh* was derived from the Latin words *solea gallica,* a Gaulish sandal. These sandals were made of wood and were attached to the foot by leather thongs crisscrossed over wrappings that reached halfway up the leg, and over the cloth shoe normally worn on dry days.

gascon/gasconade

The Basque people of the Pyrenees of northern Spain and southern France are unique. The Basques are believed to be descended from a tribe that migrated from Asia Minor and settled in the Pyrenees region at the beginning of the Bronze Age at about 2000 B.C. Their language, Basque, is the only non-Indo-European language in western Europe. It is a very ancient language that has contributed few words to English. One word that did make it, *bizarre*, means markedly unusual in appearance, style, or general character. In Basque, *bizar* meant beard, which the Spanish interpreted as energetic, manly, or brave, but which the Italians construed as unusual, also the current English definition.

Gascony is the name of the region in southern France where the French Basques lived. The word *gascon* can be traced to the Latin word *Vascon*, a Basque. These Gascons were legendary for their boastfulness. *Gascon*, therefore, became synonymous with a braggart or boaster, and *gasconade* is described as an extravagant boaster or vainglorious fiction.

Geechee. See **Gullah.**

Georgia cracker

Although the state of Georgia is officially known as the Empire State of the South, it is more popularly known as the *Peach*, *Goober* (peanut), or *Cracker State*. The peach and goober sobriquets are borne of the fact that both are major crops in the state. The reason for the *cracker* moniker is a bit more complicated.

There are several explanations for the *cracker* nickname. The *Oxford English Dictionary* (OED) cites this 1766 reference, "crackers, a name they have gotten from being boasters." Shakespeare himself employed *crackers* in the sense of a boaster in

King John. Others suggest that a *cracker* is shortened from *corn-cracker*, a device or person who cracked corn. Cracked corn was the main staple of the poor people of the shore who were also called "Sandhillers," "Low Downers," and "Poor White Trash." The final possible explanation for *cracker* is that it relates to a piece of buckskin attached to a whip, used in the region, that caused it to make a loud cracking sound. *Cracker* was used as a nickname to describe the poor people of the Carolinas, Virginia, Maryland, and especially Georgia.

The people of Georgia no longer go *crackers*, a British idiom meaning crazy, when this term is applied to them, because the *cracker* name is now considered to be fashionable.

ghetto

Here is another word that comes from an island in Venice (near the **Rialto**). Unlike the Rialto, however, this island has developed a very negative sense. Today, a *ghetto* denotes any section of a city, usually a poor one, populated predominantly by members of any particular ethnic minority. In an earlier time, though, a *ghetto* was a section of any European city inhabited exclusively by Jews.

The first *ghetto* was founded on Il Geto, the nickname of a Venetian island that was at one time the site of a canon foundry. The origin of *geto* or *ghetto* was the Latin word *jactare*, to cast or throw. In 1516, the city fathers of Venice decreed that all of the city's Jews must live on that island.

Jews started emigrating to Europe in about A.D. 70. It was a common practice for them to live together in separate communities; in this way they could maintain their cultural traditions. Pope Paul IV made it official when he decreed in 1555 that Jews living in the Papal States (around Rome) must live in separate areas. The practice spread throughout European cities, and these Jewish quarters came to be known as *ghettos* after the original one in Venice. Today, however, a *ghetto* segregates people by income and ethnicity rather than by religious persuasion.

Gibraltar

It would be difficult to place a dollar value on the British Crown Colony of Gibraltar even though the symbol for the dollar ($) is, according to popular theory, derived from this strategic piece of military real estate. Although Gibraltar is a mere 1.75 square miles, its value is based on its important location at the western end of the Mediterranean Sea, the gateway to the Atlantic Ocean. Its name is derived from the name of an Arab leader, Tarik, who conquered this impregnable fortress also known today as the Rock. The Rock's name combines *Jibal* and *Tarik,* Arab words literally meaning Tarik's Mountain, which were later anglicized to *Gibraltar*. *Gibraltar* has also come to mean any person or thing that has strength, endurance, and can be relied on.

Gibraltar also figures in the origin of the dollar sign, according to widely accepted belief. It can be traced back to a coin minted in Mexico City in 1732 which had a broken "8" or "S" for Spain and two vertical pillars. These pillars, which later became the vertical strokes of the dollar sign, represented the two pillars of Hercules or gates of the Straits of Gibraltar. The coins were called reals or pieces of eight because they were divisible into eight bits. Prior to the minting of U.S. money, the pieces of eight were widely circulated in the British colonies. A piece of a real or bit had a value of 12.5 percent of a real, or 12 and one-half cents, and two bits was worth 25 percent of a real and to this day is worth 25 cents.

The dollar is not as strong as it once was. In fact, the dollar sign today is represented on typewriters and computers with a single stroke instead of the original two pillars.

Gotham/Gothamite

Gotham is a tiny village in Nottinghamshire, England, that became proverbial for its foolish inhabitants, the *Gothamites*. The legend that influenced the special toponymous usage of this placename also inspired U.S. author Washington Irving to call New York City *Gotham*. This nickname was used for the city long before it picked up its current sobriquet, **The Big Apple** in 1972.

In a book entitled *Salmagundi* (1807–1808), Irving sarcastically nicknamed New York *Gotham* because of "the know-it-all attitude of its residents." Irving was aware of the legend of the original *Gothamites* of Nottinghamshire. According to that legend, in the fourteenth century King John of England visited *Gotham* where he had planned to build a castle. The good folk of *Gotham*, afraid that the King's presence in their town would bring about restrictions and higher taxes, conspired to act like lunatics. The objective of their plan was to convince the king, by their eccentricity, that *Gotham* was unfit to be used as the site of a royal residence. There was real method in their madness.

Gothic/Gothic art/ Gothic architecture/ gothic novel

The art and architecture of western Europe from the early thirteenth to the sixteenth century was classified as *Gothic*. While this style of work is greatly admired today, the *Gothic* sobriquet was originally conceived as a derogatory term to describe work that was thought to be inspired or created by the Goths who invaded the Roman Empire in the fourth century A.D. *Gothic architecture* was characterized by pointed arches, rib vaulting, and flying buttresses. *Gothic art* is simply a chronological designation for that same time frame.

Who were the Goths? Reliable sources agree that they were a Teutonic tribe that emigrated from a region of Sweden (perhaps around Göteborg) in A.D. 100 eastward to an area roughly equivalent to modern Hungary and Romania. It was from this new homeland that they attacked the Romans. The western Goths (Visigoths) were eventually defeated by the Gauls and their people did not survive as an ethnic or national entity.

Gothic also survives in its lower-cased form to describe a condition that is barbarous or crude. A *gothic novel* is one that has a gloomy setting and features grotesque, mysterious, or brutal events.

gringo. See **bohunk.**

Grubstreet

Samuel Johnson (1709–1784) was the greatest writer of his time. In addition to writing the first great dictionary, *Dictionary of the English Language* (1747–1755), he was a prolific writer of poetry and prose, as well as a critic and brilliant wit. In his dictionary, he defined *Grubstreet* as originally "the name of a street in Moorsfield, London, much inhabited by writers of small histories, dictionaries and temporary poems; whence any mean production was called *Grubstreet*." Grub Street is no longer on the maps of London. In an act of great charity it was renamed Milton Street in 1830, but its pejorative sense of a place inhabited by **hack** writers continues to this day.

As a noun, *Grubstreet* is currently defined as something produced by a literary hack, of poor quality. As an adjective it characterizes certain freelance or hack writers or writings. Every industry has its *Grubstreet* performers. Changing their name or address will not, by itself, change the quality of their work or product.

Gullah/Geechee

When a group of people are separated for a long time from the larger body of people speaking the same language, the smaller group invariably develops a distinctive dialect. History is full of such incidents, from the ancient people of Solei (see **Solecism**) to the blacks living on the Sea Islands off the coast of Georgia and along the eastern coast from Georgetown, South Carolina, to the northern coast of Florida. There are 250,000 people speaking this Creole language, which is called *Gullah* or *Geechee.*

Language experts have traced this special patois to two West African tribal names: Gola, the name of the original inhabitants of Liberia; and the Ngola, the name of the Angolan people. Many of the words and grammatical features of the Gullah dialect are derived from these African roots. This special jargon is also known as *Geechee,* a name derived from the Ogeechee River in Georgia. Recent studies indicate that traces of the Gullah or West African languages can also be found in the general dialect of blacks living in other parts of the United States.

Well, as they say in Gullah, "Me duh gwine gone," figuratively meaning, "I'm out of here."

gyp/gypsy

The word *gyp,* surprisingly, started out as an ethnic slur resulting from the alleged deceitful dealings of Gypsies, a group of people whose ethnic origins have been carefully traced. Both words, *gyp* and *Gypsy,* are abbreviated derivations of the Middle English word, *Egypcian.* This came about because of the mistaken belief that *Gypsies* originally came from Egypt. Actually, the *Gypsy* people can be reliably traced to India.

The *Gypsies* migrated westward from India to Egypt in A.D. 13 and then to Europe in A.D. 15, settling in Romania, Hungary, Spain, France, Russia, and England. Some *Gypsies* still speak a language based on the Sanskrit and Prakrit languages of ancient India, while others have adopted the language of the country in which they currently reside. The alleged dishonesty of a few *Gypsies* led to the shortened version, *gyp,* a verb that means to defraud, cheat, rob, or swindle (or a noun for the person who practices the gyp). Lower-cased, *gypsy* is used to describe someone who resembles a *Gypsy* characteristically; free and inclined to roam. A nonlicensed truck or cab is often referred to as a *gypsy* truck or cab. Finally, chorus dancers are endearingly referred to as *gypsies,* due to the fact that they roam from show to show, or audition to audition, seeking employment.

HHHHHHHHHHH**H**HHHHHHHHHHH

hackney/hack

Here is a word with a variety of meanings and derivatives, all of which were sired by a breed of horse that was first developed in *Hackney*, Middlesex, currently a borough of London, England. According to Eric Partridge, *Hackney* was derived from the Old English words *Hacus Ieg*, or Haca's Isle.

This equine variety was used primarily as a livery rental and coach horse, and because it was frequently overworked, its name became synonymous with drudgery. Its name also was transferred to the taxi carriages it dutifully pulled. *Hack* is a shortened version of *hackney*, which is used to describe an ordinary or uncreative writer, a member of a political machine, or an ordinary four-wheeled taxi. Today, in New York City, a stand for taxis is called a *hack* stand, and the city's bureau of taxi licensing is still called the *Hack Bureau*.

Hackney is also used as a verb meaning to make something commonplace, dull, or trite, something that etymology rarely does.

Hades/hades

Many placenames started out as eponyms (words that come from people's names)—for example, **Charleston** and **Bronx cheer.** In Greek mythology, *Hades* was originally the name of one of the three sons of Kronos, the brother of Zeus and Poseidon. *Hades* and his wife Persephone lived in the House of *Hades* on the shores of the river Styx. It was to that place that the souls of the dead were ferried across the river Styx by Charon, a boatman. *Hades'* name was later applied to the kingdom of the dead and it has become synonymous with hell.

The Romans adopted this concept of Greek mythology, but they substituted Pluto for *Hades*. *Hades* was certainly an unpleasant place, but not painful, as were its counterparts in the Christian, Moslem, and Jewish religions. Gehenna (from *gar* and *Hinnom,* literally the valley of Hinnom southwest of Jerusalem) came to be a symbol of Hell in the Jewish religion (Isaiah 66:24). It is probably from Gehenna that the concept of Christian Hell was developed in the New Testament as well.

Halifax, go to

A *euphemism* is a word or phrase in which an inoffensive term is substituted for one that is disagreeable. *Euphemism* combines the Greek suffix *eu,* meaning good, and *phanai,* to speak. The English language is peppered (or should we say salted) with examples of euphemistic words that have been substituted for more offensive ones in a variety of oaths. For example, *dear me* is an anglicized version of the Latin *Dio mio* meaning "my God," while the innocent appearing *jeepers creepers* is a mild form of *Jesus Christ* when used as an oath.

The word *damn* was at one time considered quite offensive in polite company, and so the word *dad* was substituted for it in such expression as *dad* (blamed, burned, gummed, etc.). *Go to Halifax*, a euphemism for "Go to Hell," is another polite form of profanity used by the English. Halifax, Nova Scotia, a seaport in southeast Canada, is actually a pleasant and picturesque place, known for its excellent fish. I, therefore, suggest that you go there, just for the halibut.

hamburger/burger

There are several competing theories to explain the origin of the *hamburger*, but some of these etymologies are simply whoppers. The most convincing explanation for the evolution of the *burger* was obtained from *500 Years of Words*, a book by William Sherk. Sherk explains that Hamburgers, citizens of Hamburg, Germany, were fond of a dish consisting of raw meat prepared with salt, pepper, and onion juice and known today as steak tartar. Indeed, it was from the steppes (treeless grassy plains) of the Soviet Union that this Tartar delicacy was brought to the important immigration port of Hamburg.

A broiled version of *hackfleisch*, chopped meat, eventually found its way to America. The *Oxford English Dictionary* (OED) credits Walla Walla, Washington, as the place where the *hamburger* made its American debut, but also attributes the modern *hamburger's* popularity to its introduction in sandwich form at the St. Louis Exposition of 1904. Neither the *hamburger* nor the city of Hamburg ever had any connection with ham. In fact, the word *Hamburg* literally means The Home City—it being once a center or home of missionary work. The *hamburger* officially returned home to the Home City in 1970 when McDonald's inaugurated its first fast-food emporium in the city that originally launched the *hamburger*.

hippopotamus

Is the *hippopotamus* toponymous? This is a borderline case, but this combination of Greek elements provided me with a delicious example of reduplication (compare fuddy-duddy, hodge-podge, etc.) The *hippopotamus* is a large herbivorous mammal that lives near the rivers and lakes of Africa and is capable of remaining under water for a considerable length of time.

The word *hippopotamus* combines the Greek words *hippos,* horse, and *potamios,* river, or literally river horse. The *potamios* element establishes the geographical habitat favored by the *hippopotamos,* as well as this word's origin. The term for these large animals was first used by Herodotus (Greek historian, ?484–425 B.C.). The *potamios* element is also found in the placename *Mesopotamia,* an ancient region in western Asia between the Tigris and Euphrates Rivers, now in Iraq. *Mesopotamia* literally means between the rivers.

hoagy

In most parts of the United States you can get a sandwich made of French bread (a loaf) split the long way and filled with lettuce, meats, cheese, and other assorted cold cuts. The name of this delicacy will vary depending on your geographical location. For instance, in New Orleans this type of sandwich is called a *poor boy;* in New York, a *hero;* in Boston and parts of the Southwest, a *grinder;* in Pittsburgh, New Jersey, and Los Angeles, a *submarine;* in Connecticut and Rhode Island, a *wedgie* or *wedge;* in Tampa, a *Cuban sandwich.* But the most intriguing name for this fast-food favorite is the *hoagy* from Philadelphia—a real mouthful.

The word *hoagy* first appeared in print in 1967, according to the *Oxford English Dictionary.* It was described as "ham, salami, provolone cheese and shredded lettuce all stuffed into a seven inch submarine roll." The most recent *Random House Dictionary* suggests that the *hoagy* might be a derivative of hog or more probably Hog Island in the Delaware River below Philadelphia, a great shipyard where the *hoagy* satisfied the big appetites of the ship workers there. Since many reference books indicate that the *hoagy* is of obscure origin (abbreviated as OOO), and since this is a book on toponyms, I have naturally adopted the Hog Island etymology.

The *hoagy* is most likely a variation of *hoggy,* a fast food apparently invented on Hog Island. Many foods are named after places of origin, including the **apple** and the **bialy.**

Hollywood/Hollywood kiss/ Hollywood corporal

In 1886, when Horace Wilcox laid out and named the town of Hollywood, California, he could not have known that his toponymical creation would one day provide the English language with several interesting slang idioms. This famous town, located between Beverly Hills and downtown Los Angeles, became the center of, and synonymous with, the movie industry which settled there in 1910. It was due to the nature of the movie industry and those associated with it that *Hollywood* was used to describe objects and clothing that are gaudy, loud, flashy, or sporty. *Hollywood* is also applied to people who are affected and insincere. Other *Tinseltown* idioms include:

Hollywood kiss has become a synonym for kiss off, itself meaning an act or instance of dismissing a person or thing.

Hollywood corporal was an acting corporal during World War II.

Tinseltown, according to Laurance Urdang's *Names and Nicknames of Places and Things,* is attributed to pianist and Hollywood celebrity Oscar Levant who used it as a derisive synonym for *Hollywood* in the 1940s. The Indo-European root of *holly,* incidentally, means to prick. You can be certain that many people have been "stuck" with the desire to achieve stardom in *Hollywood.*

Homburg/Panama/fedora/ bowler

Among the most perennially popular men's hats are the *Homburg, Panama,* and **derby.** I shall explore the history of the first two of these toponymous toppers here, but I refer you to the essay on *derby* for its etymology. I shall cap off this essay by adding the origins of two additional famous chapeaus, *fedora* and *bowler,* which, while not derived from placenames, are nonetheless of interest.

Homburg Very little is known about the origin of the *Homburg* except for the fact that it was first manufactured in Homburg, West Germany, once a fashionable health resort. The Homburg is a man's felt hat with a soft crown dented lengthwise and having a slightly rolled brim. It first appeared in 1890–1895 and was worn by HRH The Prince of Wales in 1901.

Panama The *Panama* hat was made from the jijippa plant. Most of these finely woven natural-fiber hats were made in Ecuador, Colombia, or Peru, but never in Panama. They were distributed to North America from Panama, and thus were called *Panama* hats.

fedora Worn by men and women, the *fedora* hat is made of soft felt. The crown is creased lengthwise. It owes its name to an 1882 production of a French play by Sardou entitled *Fedora,* in which a Russian princess by the name of Fedora first wore this style of hat.

bowler The *bowler* hat was named after Bealieu, a French hat maker. The hat, which was adopted by the English as a hard-shelled head gear for horsemen, was anglicized to *Bowler* (bowler). In the United States, the *bowler* was referred to as a *derby.*

This discussion on hats has been filled to the brim. I must doff (from "do off") my hat as a show of respect to Richard B. Manchester, whose book *Amazing Facts* was a major source for this piece.

honky/honkey

When lexicographers (people who compile dictionaries) lack space to describe the origins of a word, or are simply unwilling to do the necessary research, they often list it as OOO (of obscure origin) or some other similar abbreviation to indicate that the origin is unknown to them. *Honky* is often listed as OOO, but some fearless etymologists, such as the late John Ciardi, have presented a very plausible explanation of this ethnic slur. Ciardi and others suggest that *honky* is a variation of *hunky* (1895–1900), an uncomplimentary term for the Hungarian immigrants who settled in and around Chicago. The *honky* alteration occurred around the time of World War II. The blacks who had migrated from the South to work in the war plants picked up on the hunky slur, gave it their own twist, and applied it to all white people.

There is probably no connection between *honky* and *honky-tonk*. According to the *Oxford English Dictionary* the latter term first appeared as *honk-a-tonk* in 1894 and was defined as "a low place of amusement, or low burlesque show, especially where strong drink is available; a black barrelhouse (so called because of the barrels of liquor originally placed against the walls)." Eric Partridge suggests that *honky-tonk* is "a rhyming reduplication of honk; to make a honking noise." On occasion, *honkies* were known to show up at a honky-tonk. Jerry Lee Lewis and Elvis Presley, to name two, both loved the jazz beat of the typical honky-tonk music and went on to capitalize on this form of R&B music that was eventually imitated by other white musicians in the form of Rock 'n' Roll.

hooch

Like grog and booze, *hooch* is a slang word for whiskey. However, unlike grog and booze, *hooch* is a purely American idiom distilled from the tundra of the Forty-Ninth State's colorful history.

It all started with the foresightedness of the U.S. Secretary of State, William Seward, who in 1867 purchased Alaska, known then as Russian America. The purchase price, $7.2 million, was considered so exorbitant at the time that people referred to the transaction as "Seward's Folly" or "Seward's Icebox."

American soldiers were sent into the new territory in 1867, but were denied access to whiskey. An enterprising American sergeant, who knew how to distill alcohol, set up a still in a Hoochino Indian Village of Southern Alaska. Hoochino, a name for a branch of the Tlingit Tribe, means people of the strait of the grizzly bear.

By 1877, all strong liquor in the territory was being called Hoochino. By the time of the Klondike gold rush of 1896, Hoochino was shortened and lowercased to *hooch.* The word survives today as meaning any alcoholic liquor, but especially inferior or bootleg whiskey.

hooey. See **ballyhoo.**

hooker

There is strong evidence to support the contention that a district of old New York City was the source for the word *hooker*, a slang word for a prostitute. While there are several competing theories for the origin of this word, the New York source has hooked me. I shall first dispense with the competition.

Joseph Hooker was a Civil War general on the Union side. His command was known as Hooker's Brigade, and his headquarters was a thoroughly disreputable place. In fact, it was described as being like a brothel where "no self-respecting man liked to go nor decent woman could go." Alas, the Joe Hooker theory must be discarded because of the fact that the *hooker* idiomatic sense appeared before the war between the states began. Another possible source for *hooker* was the Hook (Hoek) of Holland where small English ships known as *hookers* traded with the Dutch. The Hook was well known for its wanton women who were supposedly known as *hookers*. References for this source of *hooker* are rather vague.

My choice for the origin of *hooker* is Corlear's Hook on Manhattan Island (NYC), where painted ladies were known as *hookers* in the early nineteenth century. Corlear's Hook was in the general vicinity of today's South Street Seaport. This hook-shaped piece of marshy land was filled in long ago by the ship-building industry that flourished there. The name Corlear came from Jacob Van Corlear who had a small tobacco plantation on the "hook" back in the mid-seventeenth century. Jacob was also a trumpeter at Ft. Amsterdam in the early Dutch settlement. Old Jacob would probably not blow his horn if he knew that the name of his old homestead was a very credible source of *hooker*.

IIIIIIIIIIIIIIIIIIIIIIIIIIIIIIIIIIIIIIIIIIIIIIIIIIIIIII

indigo/India ink

India was the earliest source of a dye and color that the Spanish called *indigo*. This Spanish form, in turn, came via Latin from the Greek word, *Indikos*. The dye, so named, came from various plants, especially the genus *Indigofera* (a member of the pea family). The color ranges from deep violet blue to a dark and grayish blue. It is prized for its colorfastness; it does not dissolve in water. Despite its Indian moniker, *indigo* was a major item of export by southern planters during the American colonial period. Even more surprising is the fact that it was a teenage girl who was responsible for its successful cultivation in the American colonies.

Elizabeth Lucas (1722–1793), the daughter of a southern plantation owner, successfully cultivated *indigo* plants on the family farms near **Charleston,** South Carolina. She was just 16 when her father died leaving her with the responsibility of managing his three farms. Elizabeth not only learned how to grow the *indigo* plant, but taught neighboring farmers to grow it too. As a result of her efforts, *indigo* became a major item of export from the colonies. She married Charles Pinckney. Their son, Charles Cotesworth Pinckney, became a member of the

Constitutional Convention in Philadelphia and later ran for the presidency against Jefferson and Madison.

After the Civil War, *indigo* was made synthetically from aniline, a coal-tar product, and the cultivation of *indigo*-producing plants disappeared. Elizabeth Pinckney, however, left an indelible mark on the history of the United States. In fact, she was so highly respected that George Washington volunteered to be a pallbearer at her funeral.

India ink originally came from China (circa 2600 B.C.) but was later exported to Europe from India, whence the name *India ink. India ink* is a dense black ink made by grinding lampblack with glue or gum. The paste made of this compound was dried and later mixed with water and used principally by artists for pen-and-ink drawings.

Irish wedding/Irish buggy/ Irish potato/Irish whiskey/ Irish coffee/Irish confetti

Several of the Irishisms below are somewhat derogatory, but all are listed in the various standard and special dictionaries in my library. *Ireland* and *Irish* can be traced to *Eire, Erin,* or *Ers,* Celtic words that probably were derived from the Runic *Yr,* a bow. But now to the wedding.

Irish wedding, someone has been to an was a phrase directed at a person with a black eye because of the alleged likelihood that a fight would break out at such affairs.

Irish buggy a wheelbarrow.

Irish potato was first cultivated by the South Americans and introduced to Europe in 1570. Although the potato is not Irish, it did become the main staple of the

Irish diet. In 1840, the Irish famine was caused by a disease that destroyed the potato crop. This led to a mass immigration of the Irish to the New World.

Irish whiskey a whiskey distilled in Ireland, characteristically made from barley.

Irish coffee a mixture of hot coffee and Irish whiskey, sweetened and topped with whipped cream.

Irish confetti bricks tossed by ruffians in a fight.

italics/Italian hand

The Italians of the sixteenth century were noted for their superb penmanship, among other things. So good were they at script, in fact, that the idiom, a fine *Italian hand,* was coined by the English to describe the excellent handwriting of Italian scribes. An *Italian hand* was first used to mean a standard of fine handwriting, but later it was broadened to mean subtlety or craftsmanship.

In 1501, Aldo Manuzio, a Venetian printer and founder of the Aldine (after his first name) Press, printed an edition of Virgil. The book was printed in a slanting type, developed by Manuzio, and said to be copied from an earlier script style. Since Manuzio was Italian, and because he dedicated the book to Italy, this new style of slanting print came to be known as *Italicus,* which was later anglicized to *italics.* Manuzio also is credited as the inventor of our modern system of punctuation.

The use of *italics* is indicated to a printer by a single line under a word or phrase in script, typewriting, or word processing. *Italics* are used today to indicate emphasis and to set off foreign words and phrases, and sometimes quotations.

Crescat scientia, vita excolatur: "Let knowledge increase, let life be perfected" (Motto of the University of Chicago).

JJJJJJJJJJJJJJJJJJJJJ J JJJJJJJJJJJJJJJJJJJJJ

jeans/denims/ dungarees

The names of many fabrics and, consequently, items of clothing made from them are often derived from the places where they were first woven. So, it should be no surprise that a trilogy of synonyms for *Levi's*™—*jeans, denims,* and *dungarees*—all came from the names of cities. Here is our *jeaneology* of this popular item of clothing worn *overall* the world.

The source of *jeans* was the word *Gene,* a sixteenth-century English name for *Genoa,* Italy, where this tough cloth was first made. The word *denims* comes from *Serge di Nimes,* fabric of Nimes, a city in France where a similar fabric was made. The name of this fabric, in time, was shortened to *di Nimes,* and finally to *denims.* Our third bolt in this trio of fabrics comes from Dungri, India, which gave us the *dungaree.*

No *jeaneological* study would be complete without *Levi's,* which comes from a man's name, Levis Strauss (1829–1902). In 1850, Strauss made work clothes for the workers and miners of California. *Levi's* is a trademarked name, but is often used to mean any pair of *jeans.*

jersey/jersey lightning/ Jersey dairy cattle/Jersey green/ New Jersey/The Jersey Bounce

This segment is devoted primarily to the *jersey*, a garment popular the world over. In addition, I shall briefly define a few other terms to which the J-word is associated, e.g., *Jersey lightning*, *Jersey dairy cattle*, *Jersey green*, *New Jersey*, and *The Jersey Bounce*, all defined in the glossary below. The lower-cased *jersey* is a knitted sweater or shirt made of wool, silk, nylon, or rayon. This comfortable article of clothing, characteristically soft and elastic, was originally knitted on the British Channel Isle of Jersey. The men of this isle, the largest of the Channel group (actually closer to France than Britain), were known to be excellent fishermen. They wore a distinctive buttonless jacket, now known as a *jersey*, which was especially suitable for this kind of work.

The island's name, surprisingly enough, was derived from none other than the great Roman leader, Julius Caesar, who conquered it in 54 B.C. In time, the island's name, according to Brewer, was softened from *Caesar's ey*, Caesar's Isle, to *Chesery*. *Chesery* was eventually corrupted to the present two-syllable version, *Jersey*. Here is a short glossary of Jersey terms:

Jersey lightning A slang term for applejack, which consists of brandy distilled from fermented cider.

Jersey dairy cattle A breed of cow originally unique to the Isle of Jersey, but now found all over the world.

Jersey green A slang term for a type of marijuana that apparently grows in New Jersey.

New Jersey Originally named Nuova Caesarea, the Latin name for the New Jersey granted by the Duke of York to Berkeley and Carteret in 1664 and later sold to William Penn.

The Jersey Bounce A kind of jumping music described in a song of the same name (1940).

Jerusalem artichoke/ Jordan almond

There are two varieties of *artichokes,* the globe and the *Jerusalem.* The globe artichoke is grown in California, although it is native to the Mediterranean area. Its place of origin can be determined, to a certain degree, by its name, which is from the Arabic *al,* meaning the, and *karshuf,* the historical name for this plant. It is actually the flower buds of the globe plant that are edible. As the *al karshuf* traveled westward, its name changed. For example, it was written as *articiocco* in Italian before it was anglicized to *artichoke.*

The *Jerusalem artichoke* is not related to the globe variety, nor is it native to Jerusalem, but to France instead. Its name, *Jerusalem,* is actually an excellent example of folk etymology (a popular but false notion of the origin of a word). In this case, *Jerusalem* is a distortion of *girasole,* an Italian word meaning turning to the sun. For you see, the *girasole* is really a variety of sunflower, *Helianthus tuberosus,* having edible tuberous root stocks the size and shape of a potato. The Jerusalem artichokes are particularly valuable for the production of levulose sugars, which people with diabetes can eat.

The *Jordan almond* is another example of folk etymology. *Jordan* in this case is derived from an earlier word, *jardyne* meaning garden; cultivated.

jodhpurs

Jodhpur was a former state in what is now Rajasthan in northwest India. The men of *Jodhpur* wore a distinctive style of trousers that were cut loose at the top but close-fitted below the knees. These trousers were adapted by India's British overlords (eighteenth to twentieth centuries) who fashioned them into riding breeches. The word *jodhpurs* remains very popular with horse people to this day. The *jodhpur boot* or *shoe* is an ankle-high shoe that is worn with *jodhpurs;* it has a strap that encircles the ankle and buckles on the side. *Jodhpur* in Sanskrit means military town.

The word *breeches,* as in *riding breeches,* comes from the early English word *broc,* the lower rear part of the body, the buttocks. Originally, *breeches* referred to knee-length trousers (knee breeches), but later came to be used informally for all trousers. Occasionally, people get to be *too big for their breeches* (or britches) and assert themselves beyond their authority or ability. By the same token, a person who is too big for his or her *jodhpurs* will probably cause a breach in his or her breeches.

Jordan almond. See **Jerusalem artichoke.**

KKKKKKKKKKKKKKKKKKKKKK

Karakul/karakul(caracul)/astrakhan/Persian

A *lamb* is a slang word for someone who is easily victimized, which is the case for the various lambs featured in this section. A *lamb* is also a young sheep whose skin is highly prized by people the world over, a fact that is sure to make the fur fly for some readers. According to the *World Book Encyclopedia,* lamb skins are sold as *broadtail, Persian,* or *astrakhan,* and *karakul* or *caracul. Broadtail* is the most expensive because of its silky, rippled appearance. It is derived from the skins of lambs that are prematurely born. *Caracul,* on the other hand, is the wavy fur of lambs that are less than two months old.

The *karakul* sheep are native to the Karakul Lake Pamir plateau in the U.S.S.R. *Karakul* combines *Kara,* meaning black, and *Kul,* lake, literally "black lake." *Astrakhan* is the fur of young lambs from Astrakhan, also in the Soviet Union at the mouth of the Volga River. It is a lustrous, closely curled wool. *Persian* lamb is strangely defined as the young lamb of the *Karakul* sheep. All of these furs are highly prized in making hats, coats, and trimming for clothing.

Kentish fire

Daniel O'Connell (1775–1847) was an Irish statesman who is known in England as "The Liberator." O'Connell formed the Catholic Association in 1823 to help English Roman Catholics of Irish descent to gain political posts. In 1828, his constituency elected him to the English Parliament, but the English laws in effect at the time forbade members of the Catholic Church to hold public office. All that changed when the Catholic Emancipation Act (Catholic Relief Bill) was passed in 1829, enabling O'Connell to take his seat in that great English institution, Parliament.

There was a great deal of opposition to the Catholic Relief Bill, the legislation that would give equal rights to Catholics. In Kent, a county in southeastern England encompassing Canterbury and Dover, the people expressed their opposition to this proposed legislation by prolonged clapping and foot stamping, which made it impossible for those supporting the bill to speak. This ironic form of applause was called *Kentish fire*.

Kentish fire remains in use today and is defined as prolonged clapping by an audience, especially in unison, indicating impatience or disapproval. Such expressions of censure are usually orchestrated to prevent a speaker from talking. It did not, however, help the Kentish folk in their effort to thwart the passage of the Catholic Relief Bill.

LLLLLLLLLLLLL**L**LLLLLLLLLLLLL

laconic/spartan

During the Battle of the Bulge in World War II, an American officer, General McAuliffe, responded to a German demand to surrender with the very terse response, "Nuts!" More than two thousand years earlier, a leader of Sparta responded in an equally brief manner to this threat by Phillip of Macedonia: "If I enter Laconia, I will level Sparta [the capital city] to the ground." The Spartan's answer was simply, "If."

Laconia is a region of ancient Greece on the Peloponnesus where the citizens were known to be very sparing with words. This resulted in an English adjective, *laconic,* which means brief or terse in speech. A *spartan* is another word inspired by the legendary traits of the Laconian's who were warlike, brave, hardy, **stoical,** severe, and frugal. It is good to have such a person on your side in battle, but otherwise B-O-R-I-N-G.

landau/landaulet

Vehicle styles often take their names from the places where they were first produced—for example, **limousine** and **coach.** The *landau* and *landaulet* were first made in Landau, Bavaria, West

Germany, in 1735–1745. The German name for this carriage was *landauer wagen,* which was shortened to *landau.* This style of carriage was very popular in the eighteenth century.

The original *landau* was a four-wheel closed carriage with front and back seats that faced each other, and a roof in two sections that could be folded back. The *landaulet* was similar to the *landau,* but was a one-seater. The *landau* name was later transferred to a sedanlike automobile with a short convertible back seat. The closest thing to the *landau* at the present time is the stretch **limousine** which has facing seats in the back compartment and a large sunroof that can be opened electrically.

Lesbian/lesbian

There is a place on this planet where both men and women are called *Lesbians*—with a capital "L." That place, of course, is Lesbos in the eastern Aegean Sea off the northwest coast of Turkey where the people are quite naturally known as *Lesbians.* This same word, spelled with a lower-cased "l," has also come to refer to a woman who is homosexual. (The *homos* element in this word is often confused with the Latin word *homo,* meaning man, but is actually derived from Greek and means same. They combine to literally mean same sex.) How did the name of the people of this hilly island deviate from its original meaning? Here is the not so lurid story behind *lesbian.*

The use of *lesbian* in its sexual connotation is attributed to Sappho, who was born on Lesbos in 612 B.C. She was a poetess and a leader of the group of young women and girls who were dedicated to the cult of Aphrodite. She expressed great affection for these women, and tongues have been wagging ever since. Some of her poems were copied by the Greek poet Horace, and Sappho is considered by many scholars to be one of the world's greatest poets.

lethargy/lethal

Many English words are derived from mythological places and people. *Lethargy,* which has come to mean the quality or state of being drowsy and dull, listless and unenergetic, or indifferent and lazy, is such a word, having been derived from the ancient religion of classical Greece. In this religion, now considered myth, the river **Hades** was fed by five rivers, one of which was the Lethe. It was in the Lethe that a person's spirit was immersed to wash away the memory of its life on earth.

Greek medical physicians later coined the word *lethargia* to characterize certain illnesses in which a person is extremely drowsy. This was the basis for the current English word *lethargy.* The Roman interpretation of the Lethe myth was that lasting forgetfulness only came with death, and they coined the word *lethalis,* which was eventually anglicized as *lethal,* meaning deadly or fatal.

Lilliputian/Brobdingnagian

Literature is the source of many fictional toponyms that enrich our language. This was certainly the case with Jonathan Swift's (1667–1745) popular book, *Gulliver's Travels* (1726), considered a masterpiece of literature. This unusual travelog described the voyages of Lemuel Gulliver, a ship's doctor who journeyed to very strange lands. Gulliver's first stop was Lilliput, where the people were one-twelfth his size. Lemuel helped these tiny people who treated him very well at first, but later turned against him. His second voyage brought him to Brobdingnag where the people were 12 times his size and greatly amused by his *Lilliputian* size.

Lilliputian is currently defined as extremely small, tiny, or diminutive. It can also describe someone who is narrow or petty in outlook. Swift's creativity also resulted in the word

Brobdingnagian, an antonym for *Lilliputian*. This English author was born in Dublin, Ireland. In 1694 he became a minister and later Dean of St. Patrick's in Dublin. His *Brobdingnagian* literary production is all the more surprising when one realizes the nature of his work while writing his humorous and often bitter satire.

limerick

A *limerick* is a humorous verse named after the city of Limerick, Ireland, with which it has long been identified. A typical *limerick* has five lines in which the first two lines rhyme with the fifth, while the third and fourth lines rhyme with each other. Credit for collecting and publishing one of the first anthologies of this poetic form is attributed to Englishman Edward Lear (1812–1888) of *The Owl and The Pussycat* fame. This delightful children's book, written and illustrated by Lear in 1871, is a favorite of generations of children and was the source of the **runcible spoon.**

The *limerick* was first introduced to the world in Lear's 1846 book entitled *A Book of Nonsense,* which was a collection of such ditties. At one time these *limericks* were also called *learics* after Edward Lear. Lear was not from Limerick, Ireland, a city that lies on both sides of the Shannon River, but from the vicinity of London. The *Encyclopedia Britannica* suggests that the *limerick* style originated in France and was brought back to Ireland by returning soldiers. Here is an example of the *limerick,* courtesy of the *Britannica:*

> A tutor who taught on the flute
> tried to teach two young tooters to toot.
> Said the two to the tutor,
> "Is it harder to toot, or
> To tutor two tooters to toot?"

limousine/limo

In the central western province of Limousin, France, shepherds wore a traditional hooded costume that became known as a *limousine*. This same word was later used to describe a type of horse-drawn vehicle having a permanently closed compartment for three to five people with a roof projecting forward over the driver's seat in front. The hooded front compartment of this early sedan (1900–1905) was apparently similar to the hooded *limousine* garment. The chief town of Limousin Province, Limoges, is now best known for its fine porcelain china.

The word *limousine* has been generalized to describe any large and luxurious auto, especially one driven by a chauffeur. Today's *limousine* has not only lost its hood but its last syllable, *-sine*, as it is now more popularly known as a *limo*.

linsey-woolsey. See **worsted.**

lumber

Long ago, a northern German tribe known as the *Longobardus*, a name that literally means long beards, invaded northern Italy and set up a kingdom there. The Longobardus, who later became known as *Lombards*, gained renown throughout Europe for their success as pawnbrokers. In fact, there is a Lombard Street in modern-day London, England, where the Lombards first established their English headquarters many years earlier. Lombard Street remains a financial center to this day. One of the most famous Lombard families were the Medici of Florence, Italy.

By the seventeenth century, *lombard* had been anglicized to *lumber*, which in turn, had come to mean timber. This sense change had probably come about because the typical *lombard* yards were strewn with old barrel staves and miscellaneous pieces of wood and assorted junk that could be purchased there. The *lombard* yard was ultimately eased into *lumber* yard.

The word *lumber* also means to move clumsily, or trudge, as in "we're nearing the end of this *lumbering* essay." This second *lumber* comes from the Swedish word *lomra* meaning to resound or walk heavily and is not related to the financially swift Lombards.

lush/lushy/lusher/lushhead

Today, a *lush* or alcoholic is someone to be pitied, but at one time (1895) a *lush* was a member of a venerable actors' drinking club, The City of Lushington, in London. This ebrius group, which met at the Harp Tavern on Russell Street, had a Lord Mayor who jokingly lectured new members on the evils of strong drink. The City also had four aldermen appropriately named Juniper, Poverty, Lunacy, and Suicide.

According to Brewer, Lushington was the name of an old London brewery that must go back a long way, since the word *lush* first appeared in print in 1795. Other derivatives from The City of Lushington include: *lushy,* drunk or tipsy; and *lusher* and *lushhead,* both meaning drunkard. This drinking society is now out of commission, but its four aldermen (Juniper, Poverty, Lunacy, and Suicide), like The Four Horsemen of the Apocalypse (Conquest, War, Famine, and Death) are still stalking the land in search of new victims.

lyceum

In the piece on **Chatauqua,** I briefly discussed the American *lyceum* movement that got started in 1826. The popularity of this American cultural circuit spread rapidly and featured such speakers as Ralph Waldo Emerson (1803–1882), Henry David Thoreau (1817–1862), Daniel Webster (1782–1852), Henry Ward

Beecher (1804–1864), and Susan B. Anthony (1820–1906). The word for this lecture series, *lyceum,* had its toponymous origin in ancient Greece during the Aristotelian period. Return with me to Ancient Greece to learn more about *lyceum* and the great philosophers.

One of Plato's keenest students at his **academy** near Athens was Aristotle (384–322 B.C.), himself a great philosopher, scientist, and educator. Aristotle, like Plato, set up his own school which became known as a *lyceum.* This nickname for Apollo, *Lyceum,* was derived from *Lukeios,* representing either Lycia (the god) in Asia Minor (Turkey) or the wolf (-killer) from the Greek word for wolf, *lukos.* The Lyceum was a courtlike space bounded by buildings which became a gymnasium for Greek athletes. It got its name from the temple of Apollo (Lukeion) that dominated the area. It was here that Aristotle would, as Plato did at the Academy, lecture those who would listen while he strolled around the paths of that ancient religious, academic, and sports center. Aristotle's institute was known as the *peripatetic* (a word derived from a Greek word meaning walking around) *school.*

Aristotle's fame as a brilliant student and teacher was so great that he was retained by King Phillip of Macedonia to teach his son, who grew up to become Alexander the Great. It was after his tour as Alexander's tutor that Aristotle returned to Athens to set up shop at the Lyceum. After Alexander's death, Aristotle, like Socrates before him, got into trouble with his fellow Athenians because of his alleged lack of piety for the gods. Unlike Socrates, Aristotle was never brought to trial, because he left his post at the Lyceum for the city of Chalcis where he died a year later. Today, a *lyceum* is a hall in which public lectures, concerts, and similar programs are presented, or any organization presenting such programs.

MMMMMMMMMMMMMMMMMMM

macassar/antimacassar

In the early nineteenth century, when men commonly used grooming oils on their hair, homemakers found it necessary to develop defenses against this greasy kid stuff that stained their upholstered furniture. The result is the word *antimacassar,* which is still in use and defined as "a small covering, usually ornamental, placed on the backs and arms of upholstered furniture to prevent wear or soiling; also called a *tidy.*"

The *Macassar* that they were trying to protect against was an oil (unguent) for the hair distributed by Roland & Son early in the nineteenth century. The oil was extracted from the *Schleichera trijuga* plant which was exported from the port of Makassar in the Celebes Islands, Indonesia. Later, a mixture of coconut oil and ylang-ylang extract was substituted for the real McCoy, er, *Macassar.*

macedoine

The desire for ethnic independence has been a major cause for war and unrest between nations, and even between people of the same nation, throughout history. Humans seem to exhibit a strong need to identify with those within their society who have the same language, religion, culture, and physical features. This need to flock together provides a sort of security blanket, but often leads to physical violence even today. This phenomenon can be observed between the Basques (see **gascon**) and their Spanish countrymen, among the people having cultural and religious differences in the Middle East, among the many neighboring ethnic cultures of the Soviet Union, as well as among the people of ancient Macedonia in what is now the Balkan Peninsula. (See **Balkanization,** where there is a real *macedoine* of people.)

The Balkans is a region in southern Europe including Greece, Bulgaria, and Yugoslavia. This area was, at one time, ruled by Phillip of Macedoine (Macedonia) and his son, Alexander the Great. The Balkans, nee Macedonia, has such a mixture of people that *macedoine* figuratively came to mean a mixture of fruit or vegetables often served as a salad, or, simply a medley.

Mackinaw/Mackinaw blanket/ Mackinaw boat

Mackinac Island is a beautiful vacation spot in Lake Huron at the entrance to the Straits of Mackinac. The Straits separate northern Michigan from southern Michigan and divide Lakes Huron and Michigan. The Straits are crossed by a suspension bridge with one of the world's longest center spans (3,800 feet) and which has a total length of 7,400 feet. The bridge was completed in 1957. The only means of transportation on this island, where automobile traffic is banned, is the horse and buggy.

The island was the site of a trading post where a short double-breasted coat of thick woolen plaid material was sold (1755–1765). The coat became known as a *mackinaw*. Later, the *Mackinaw blanket* (1882) and the *Mackinaw boat* (1883) also took their names from the island. *Mackinac* is derived from an Algonquin Indian word, *michilmackinac,* a large turtle after the shape of the island.

The *mackinaw* should not be confused with a *macintosh,* a raincoat made of rubber-sized cloth, and named after Charles Mackintosh (1776–1843), its British inventor.

Madison Avenue/Mad Ave

English-speaking people have a penchant for abbreviating words or phrases. *Madison Avenue,* once the most popular address for advertising firms, is a good example of this kind of verbal telescoping. *Madison Avenue* has, in its relatively short life, already been shortened to *Mad Ave.* The long and short versions of this street name are used colloquially and collectively as a nickname for American advertising agencies and the ad industry. It is a common practice the world over for industries to congregate in one district or street—for example, Lombard Street (see **lumber**), Corlear's Hook (see **hooker**), and **Wall Street.** *Madison Avenue* is simply another example of the clustering inclinations of many industries.

The dating of a word's (or idiom's) initial usage is commonly determined by its first appearance in print. In this case, we have a twelve-year difference of opinion. The *Oxford English Dictionary* records its first appearance in print in H. Kurnitz' *Invasion of Privacy* (1956): ". . . dressed in the dark grey neat stripes of a *Madison Avenue* advertising executive." Morris, however, cites an earlier (1944) usage. Despite the fact that New York ad agencies have been widely dispersed to other New York locations in recent years (Third, Fifth, Sixth, and Park Avenues), the *Madison Avenue* idiom has gained what appears to be a permanent and overwhelming market share as a toponymous sobriquet for the entire industry.

maelstrom

There was a time when sea travel was far more hazardous than it is today. The volume of treasure and artifacts recovered from ancient shipwrecks can attest to that. Wind-powered ships were always at the mercy of unpredictable weather and navigational hazards. One such place that combined the twin hazards of a whirlpool and land was **Scylla and Charybdis.** So infamous were the dangers of another famous whirlpool, located in the Arctic Ocean off the coast of Norway, that it was given the nickname *maelstrom,* a Dutch word that literally means stream that grinds. Such places were probably the basis for numerous legends of sea monsters that could reach out and sink any ship that came within their grasp.

This windy old terror, *maelstrom,* has taken on an idiomatic sense and is currently defined as a restless, disorderly state of affairs or any overpowering force or far-reaching influence.

Maffick

World War II officially ended on August 15, 1945, the day Japan accepted the allied surrender terms. This date is remembered as V-J day (Victory over Japan day). Anyone old enough to remember that day will never forget the spontaneous public displays of joy. And so it was for the English when the news reached London that the Boer siege of Mafeking had been lifted after 217 days—from October 12, 1899, to May 17, 1900.

Mafeking is a town in the North Republic of South Africa that at one time was the administrative seat of Bechwanaland (now Botswana). It was the scene of a critical battle during the second Boer War fought between the Dutch Boers (farmers) and the English settlers. The British broke the siege and went on to win the war. The victory sparked extravagant celebrations in London and inspired the nonce word *maffick,* a verb meaning to celebrate with extravagant public demonstrations. *Nonce* is derived from the Middle English words *nones,* resulting from the faulty division of *then ones.* A *nonce word* is one coined and used only for a particular occasion.

magenta

From A.D. 306 to 312, a Roman general, Marcus Maxentius, established his headquarters in a town in northern Italy west of Milan. The name of this now colorful town, Magenta, is a corruption of the old general's last name. Over 1,500 years passed before this *eponym* (a word from a person's name) cum toponym came to be used for a color that was first developed there, *magenta,* a purplish-red color. It is ironic that another general also had a hand in this color transfer.

In 1859, the French and Sardinians under the command of Napoleon III defeated the Austrians at the Battle of Magenta. The battle was historically significant because it led to Italian independence. In that same year, while the blood of nine thousand soldiers stained the land, a new dye was developed in Magenta. It was named for its place of origin, as are many other commodities, and undoubtedly because of the battle fought there as well. Perhaps *magenta* became symbolic of the blood that was spilled on that battlefield.

magnet/milk of magnesia

This word has a strong attraction for many, like the country from whence it was first discovered, Greece. The Greek name for the magnetic stones was *he Magnesia lithos* or the stones of Magnesia. Magnesia is a district in Thessaly, Greece, where these attractive stones were first mined. Today, of course, a *magnet* is a piece of iron or steel that attracts other ferrous metals.

Few people, however, are attracted to milk of magnesia, a

milky-white fluid of magnesium hydroxide suspended in water and used as a laxative.

malaguena/Malaga

We are about to add *malaguena* to our terpsichorean collection of words that includes the **Charleston, flamenco,** and **tarantella.** *Malaguena* is a dance of Malaga, the name of a province and its capital city in the Andalusian region of southern Spain. Vacationers would recognize Malaga as part of the Costa del Sol, while art lovers would identify this city as the birthplace of Pablo Picasso. This beautiful city was founded by the Phoenicians (see **Punic faith**) in the twelfth century B.C. It was held by the Romans and Visigoths, taken by the Moors in 711, reconquered by Ferdinand and Isabella in 1487, and occupied by the French from 1810 to 1812. The name *Malaga* is of Phoenician origin and, according to etymologist Adrian Room, probably meant queen.

One of Malaga's principal exports is *Malaga* wine, a strong, sweet dessert wine with a pronounced muscat grape flavor. Malaga's dance export, the *Malaguena,* is a lively Spanish dance similar to the *fandango,* which in turn is a dance in triple time performed by a man and woman playing castanets. *Fandango* has developed the sense of a boisterous assembly, and has also inspired the slang word *fandangle* which is defined as an ornament, mechanical object, or a profuse confusion.

mall/pell-mell/Pall Mall/ pall-mall

"When the door opened, the crowd rushed *pell-mell* into the *mall* on *Pall Mall* to watch a game of *pall-mall.*" This sentence combines all of the words that can be traced back to the once popular game of *pall-mall* (pronounced pel-mel) that originated in Italy during the seventeenth century. This game eventually gave its name to a street from which today's enclosed shopping centers or *malls* were named. Put your credit cards away, because this visit to the *mall* will not cost you a cent.

The source of all of these featured words is the Italian game of *pallamaglio,* or mallet ball. The game, which the English call *pall-mall,* was first played on a grassy alley in Rome at the end of which was mounted a high arched iron hoop. The purpose of the game was to see who could hit a wooden ball *(palla)* with a wooden mallet *(maglio)* through the metal arch most often. The game was adopted by the English who first played it on St. James Place in London. The street was later named after the game played there, and to this day is still known as *Pall Mall.*

Pall-mall, the game, was the source of, or at least influenced the idiom, *pell-mell,* a common twentieth-century expression meaning in disorderly, headlong haste or in a reckless hurried manner. *Pell-mell* was suggestive of the helter-skelter manner in which participants in *pall-mall* rushed after the ball.

While *pall-mall* and *pell-mell* preceded *Pall-Mall,* the word *mall* was named after the old *pall-mall* field that became the street called *Pall Mall. Pall-mall* was shortened to *mall* and in the eighteenth century became synonymous with tree-lined walks. New York and Boston had such *malls* in the early 1800s.

In the 1970s, American architects began to promote pedestrian *malls,* and only then was the word *mall* applied to enclosed shopping centers in general. The credit for creating the first enclosed shopping center also goes to the Italians. The first such structure, I am told, was the Galleria in Milan, Italy, which was built in the nineteenth century and is still sheltering shoppers from around the world. Incidentally, Eric Partridge traces the word *gallery* to the Latin *galilea,* a vestibule or minor porch of a church. This is altogether appropriate, for *mall* shopping seems to be a kind of twentieth-century religion for many. *Galilea,* according to Eric Partridge, can be traced to the scriptural Galilee of the Gentiles, which makes the word *gallery* a toponym.

Maltese cross, cat, dog/ Malta Summit/Malta, Knights of

The Malta meeting (a nonsummit summit) between Presidents Mikhail Gorbachev of the Soviet Union and George Bush of the U.S. at Marsaxlokk Bay, Malta, in late 1989 brought Malta into the news again. Malta is an island in the Mediterranean Sea between Sicily and Africa. This former British colony, now a member of the British Commonwealth of Nations, has a population of about 370,000 people on 95 square miles. During its long history, the island was colonized by the Phoenicians in 1000 B.C., and conquered by the Romans, Byzantines, Saracens, Knights of St. John (also known as the Knights Hospitaller, Knights of Malta, or Knights Templar), French, and English. *Malta* is derived from the Arabic word *Malita* which means either a place of refuge or is the name of Malta's ethnic deity. Here are several items associated with *Malta:*

Maltese cross a cross having four equal arms that expand in width at their tips to provide eight points. It was adopted by the Knights of St. John when they fought in the Crusades.

Maltese cat a bluish-gray variety of domestic cat first bred on Malta.

Maltese dog one of a breed of dogs having a long, straight, silky white coat.

The Knights Templar, who claim to be descended from the medieval order of Templar, is a Masonic order in the United States. The Templars got their name from the fact that their military headquarters in the twelfth century was located near the Jewish temple in Jerusalem. The site of the *Malta Summit*, once the home of the Knights *Hospitaller*, proved to be in*hospitable* as a result of the storm that raged during that historic event.

Manhattan cocktail

Etymology is not an exact science. Often, the origin of a word or phrase is developed by sifting through the evidence and making the most logical conclusion(s) as to its source. In the case of the *cocktail,* I have screened the evidence and will present the results of my research.

The *cocktail* is any of various alcoholic drinks made of a distilled liquor mixed with wine, fruit juice, and the like, and usually iced. My judgment is that *cocktail* is most likely derived from the French word *coquetier,* an egg cup, in which a New Orleans apothecary, Antoine Peychaud, mixed and served tonics. The name of the serving cup, *coquetier,* was eventually transferred to the drink and then eased to *cocktail.* This theory is reinforced by American author Washington Irving, who in 1809 wrote about "those recondite beveridges, cock-tail, stone-fence, and sherry cobbler." Irving's comment seems to support the *coquetier* explanation since at that early date (1809) *cocktail* was still used to describe a specific drink and not as a general term for all alcoholic concoctions.

According to one noted authority, the *Manhattan cocktail* was invented by a bartender at the Manhattan Club in New York City in the 1870s. As a New Yorker, my drink should be the Manhattan—except for the fact that I am a *teetotaller,* someone who abstains from alcoholic beverages. Richard Turner, an Englishman, claims to have coined the word *teetotaller* in the 1830s and even had it inscribed on his tomb.

Manila

Give an etymologist enough rope and he will invariably search for their word origins, especially if they are derived from a placename such as *Manila. Manila* is the capital of the Philippines (named after Philip II of Spain) on southwest Luzon. As is so often the case, *Manila* products got their names from the place where they were first or principally exported. Other examples include **macassar, dollar,** and **bayonet.**

Manila rope comes from the abaca plant grown in the Philippines. It grows 20 feet high, has oblong leaves, and is similar in appearance to the banana tree to which it is related. The hard, strong fibers come from the leaf stems of the abaca. The ropes made from these fibers were particularly resistant to wind, water, and sun, and were the best that money could buy—that is, until ropes made of nylon became available. *Manila* fibers were, at one time, also used in the manufacture of a very strong paper known as *manila,* which was used for heavy-duty envelopes and other paper products. And although such products are now made of wood fibers, any paper resembling the light brown or buff color of the original are still referred to as *manila.*

marathon

"Rejoice! We have conquered!" These words were the last ever spoken by Phidippides, a Greek messenger, after running from the plains of Marathon to tell his countrymen in Athens of their great victory over the Persians in 490 B.C. Shortly after delivering his message, Phidippides fell dead from exhaustion.

Phidippides' heroic run was commemorated by a race named the *marathon* which was added to the Olympic games in 1896. In the British Olympics of 1908, the *marathon* began at Windsor Castle and finished in front of the king's box in London's Olympic stadium. The distance was 26 miles 385 yards, the standard distance of most *marathons* to this day.

The plain where this historic battle raged was covered with fennel (parsley family) for which the Greek word is *marathon.* And while the word *marathon* has nothing to do with running or endurance, the *-athon* element is nonetheless added to English words to indicate that such an event is intensive or of long endurance (e.g., *sellathon, telethon*).

Marengo, chicken

There are three homophonic words (those that sound similar but have different meanings)—*Marengo, meringue,* and *merengue*—two of which will delight your gustatorial senses while the third will add gusto to your dancing pleasure. Only one of these, *Marengo,* is a toponym and I shall, therefore, dish that word out to you first.

Marengo is a village in northwest Italy's Lombardy Plains where Napoleon Bonaparte defeated the Austrians on June 14, 1800. The victory gave France undisputed control of the Milan region and greatly increased Napoleon's prestige with the French people. It has also delighted gourmets who now enjoy a French dish, *chicken Marengo,* which was inspired by this important French triumph. It consists of chicken browned in oil and cooked with tomatoes, garlic, wine, mushrooms, and brandy.

Another homophonous delicacy is *meringue,* a delicate frothy mixture made with beaten egg whites, sugar, and hot syrup, then browned, and used as a topping. This is of French origin but unknown etymology.

Our final soundalike is *merengue,* a ballroom dance of Dominican or Haitian origin, and the music for this dance, also of unknown origin.

A perfectly homophonic evening could be spent dining on *chicken Marengo,* followed by a lemon *meringue* pie, after which one would work off the calories while dancing the *merengue.* Now that sounds like a full evening.

marijuana/Maui wowie/ Acapulco gold

How did such nice placenames as Maui, an island in the Hawaiian Islands, Acapulco on the Pacific coast of Mexico, and Mariguana Island in the Bahamas come to be associated with the narcotic derived from the hemp plant? Take a trip (an etymological journey) with me as I trace the source of these terms.

marijuana a Mexican slang word for the dried leaves and female flowers of the hemp plant used in cigarette form as a narcotic or hallucinogen. Excellent authorities believe that the origin of this word or plant may have been Mariguana, one of the islands in the Bahamas. This hemp product, now spelled *marijuana,* is also called Maria Juana south of the border and Mary Jane in the U.S.

Maui wowie a species of *marijuana* that is highly sought after because of its higher content of hallucinogens. Maui is the second largest island in the Hawaiian Islands.

Acapulco gold another form of *marijuana* grown in Mexico and also prized for its high hallucinogenic content.

Martello tower

On one of my frequent vacations in England I was driving along the beautiful English Channel coast where I was first introduced to the *Martello towers*. These fortified towers (74 in all) were erected by order of the Duke of York in 1803 as a defense against a feared invasion by Napoleon Bonaparte of France. The *towers* are 30 to 40 feet in height with walls 9 feet thick and surrounded by deep ditches. In addition to the English, the French, Canadians, and Americans have at one time erected similar fortlike structures. Each *Martello tower* was armed with guns at its top.

The *Martello tower* was named after Cape Mortella, Corsica, where a prototype of this kind of tower was besieged and finally captured by the British. In this battle, the British were fighting in support of the Corsicans against the French. The towers along the English coast were erected because of the fear of reprisal by the French. These towers quickly became useless against powerful naval guns that were in use in the nineteenth century.

The *Martello towers* are monuments to the futility of war.

Maui wowie. See **marijuana.**

mayonnaise

When it comes to food preparation, most of us are Francophiles (see **frank**), because many of our favorite recipes and sauces were invented or improved upon by the French. The ancestry of these toponymous toppings is revealed by the *-aise* ending, the French suffix which means native to, or originating in that country. Among these are *mayonnaise,* hollandaise, dijonaise, and béarnaise.

The most historically intriguing of this saucy quartet is *mayonnaise* which, according to legend, was concocted by the chef of the Duc de Richelieu whose French army defeated the British at Port Mahon on the Spanish island of Minorca in 1756. At a special victory celebration feast, it is said, the Duke's chef prepared a unique new sauce which became known as *Mahonnaise,* after Port Mahon, and was later anglicized to *mayonnaise.* Port Mahon, according to tradition, was founded by the Carthaginians in 200 B.C. and was named after General Mago, the brother of Hannibal (see **Cannae** and **Punic faith**).

Mayonnaise combines egg yolks, butter, lemon juice, and seasonings. This French sauce is frequently used in salads and as a sandwich spread.

meander

This book on toponyms is *meandering* around the world like a winding river. The *meandering* metaphor is appropriate in this case, because the word *meander* was derived from a Greek river, the *Maiandros,* that wound through Asia Minor. *Meander* is defined as to proceed by or take a winding or indirect course; to wander aimlessly; ramble. It is also said that the Maiandros River was the inspiration for the ancient and classic Greek key design that graces Greek jewelry, architecture, art, and furniture.

mecca

A short distance from Jeddah, Saudi Arabia, is Mecca, the holy city of Islam and the birthplace of the prophet Mohammed in A.D. 570. It is to this city, according to the Koran, that all Moslems are required to make a raj or pilgrimage at least once during their lifetime and, therefore, Mecca is the main center of Moslem fervor. The word *mecca* is also used figuratively to mean a place that is regarded as the center of an activity or interest. For example, New York is a *mecca* for theater-goers.

Some years ago I visited Jeddah and expressed an interest in visiting Mecca. I was advised that only Moslems were allowed in the city and that there was a road that bypassed Mecca that is known as the *Infidel Road.* Apparently, Mecca is only a religious *mecca* for Moslems.

Melba toast/peach Melba/ Melba sauce

Here is a a peach of a story in which I have exercised the literary license to which I am entitled. For you see, our focus word, *Melba,* while appearing to have been derived from a person's name (such words are called *eponyms*) is, upon closer inspection, actually derived from a placename. And so, the *Melba* name, in the food sense, is an example of a toponym turned eponym.

Dame Nellie Melba (1861–1931) was a famous coloratura soprano who inspired the foods featured here. There are several versions of how *peach Melba* (also *peach melba* and *peche Melba*) was so named. There is no doubt, however, that famed French chef Georges Auguste Escoffier created it. Dame Nellie was hosting a dinner party in a hotel in which Escoffier was the chef. He created a special dessert for the occasion consisting of a cooked peach half served with vanilla ice cream and a clear raspberry sauce. The raspberry sauce is still referred to as *Melba sauce.* The success of this delightful concoction resulted from its delicious taste and the fame of Melba and Escoffier. Melba's popularity and peculiar eating habits were responsible for another food, *Melba toast,* which consists of very thin sliced toast, baked in the oven until golden brown. *Melba toast* is now generic for such toasts which are still available in grocery stores under that name.

The placename connection of *Melba* results from the fact that Dame Nellie Melba was born Helen Mitchell Porter. She took as her stage name the first element in the name of the city near where she was born, Melbourne, Australia.

millinery/millenary/Milan

Millinery and *millenary* are phononyms (words that sound alike but have different meanings). The first of these two words is, appropriately, a toponym having to do with women's topwear (hats), while *millenary* means consisting of or pertaining to a thousand, especially a thousand years.

Let's take it from the top—the *millinery* word, which is based on the name of an Italian city, Milano (Milan). In the fifteenth century, the hat makers of Milano were known for their fine straw hats which they exported throughout Europe. Soon after, Milan became a major center of hat manufacturing and the word *milliner* came to mean a person who makes, trims, or sells women's hats. *Millinery* now refers to anything having to do with the manufacture of hats. The word is becoming obsolete as the demand for women's hats has been sharply reduced in the last 30 years.

Milan is the second largest city in northwest Italy. The word *Milan* comes from an ancient word *mediolanum,* which literally means the middle of the meadow. Perhaps the *millinery* industry will revive sometime within the next millenium.

Missouri, I'm from

An extemporaneous remark made by a Missouri congressman in 1899 has not only become a slogan for the citizens of that state, but has become idiomatic for any person unwilling to accept something without proof, skeptical—I'm from Missouri and you'll have to show me that you're right.

According to Charles Funk, the expression was first uttered by Willard D. Vandiver, a member of Congress from Missouri, in his speech before the Five O'Clock Club of Philadelphia. The previous speaker had made several boastful and highly unlikely claims about the productiveness of Iowa. Vandiver, in his extemporaneous remarks preceding his speech, said, "I come from a country that raises corn, cotton, cockleburs, and Democrats. *I'm from Missouri* and you've got to show me." This statement so appealed to his fellow Missourians that they started to call themselves citizens of the *show me* state.

mocha. See **coffee.**

mogul

Some years ago a book entitled *The Moguls* was published and quickly became a best seller. It contained a series of biographies about highly successful captains of industry, explained how they got started, and described the methods they used to build their fortunes. The word *mogul* is presently defined as a very rich or powerful person. For the origin of *mogul,* we must delve into Eastern history.

The Great and Grand Mogul was the title used by Europeans for the emperor of Delhi, India, whose empire, at one time, included most of Hindustan. This Mongolian dynasty was founded in 1526 by Baber, a descendant of the Mongol Turks, Tamerlane, and Genghis Kahn. The last of these rulers was dethroned in 1857. *Mogul* is a westernized version of the Persian word *Mughul,* a Mongol, especially one of the rulers of India.

money

Brewer's *Dictionary of Phrase and Fable* published in 1870 retells the fascinating legend of the Roman goddess Juno upon whose cult name, *Moneta,* the word *money* was coined. According to Brewer, during the Gallic invasion of Rome in 390 B.C., the Romans were alerted to the invasion of the Gauls by the honking of the sacred geese kept in Juno's shrine atop the Capitoline Hill (see **capitol**). After that event, the superstitious Romans began calling Juno by a new nickname, *Moneta,* meaning little warner. Later, Lucius Furius built a temple to Juno Moneta on the Capitoline Hill (see **capitol**) to express the gratitude of the Roman people toward Juno. Juno was already quite popular, though. In addition to being the wife of Jupiter, she watched over women, protected maidenhood, was the goddess of marriage (that is why June, named after Juno, is still such a favorite month for marriage), and much more.

In 269 B.C., the temple of Juno Moneta was converted into a mint where silver coins were produced. These coins were called *Monetas,* and the Latin word *Monetarius* came to mean pertaining to money. By A.D. 1250, the English were using the word *moonay* (a possible source of the slang word for money, *moola*) as meaning coinage of the realm. It had entered English via the old French word *moneie. Mint,* the place where coins were minted, also descended from the original mint of Juno Moneta.

moon, shoot the/ minions of the moon/ man in the moon/moonshine/ moonroof/moonlight/blue moon/ moonies/moony/moonstruck

The *moon* is the earth's natural satellite orbiting the earth at an average distance of 238,857 miles. In the language of the Anglo-Saxons, the word for moon, *mona,* was also defined as a measure of time. In fact, the old English word for month, *monath,* a period of approximately 30 days, is also derived from *mona.* The *moon* has figured heavily in religions, prose and poetry, superstitions, and, of course, languages. So here is our collection of *phrases* of the moon.

shoot the moon to go all out; to be very ambitious; to aim at the moon.

minions of the moon thieves who rob by night.

man in the moon Shakespeare *(A Midsummer Night's Dream)* and Numbers 15:32–36 from the Bible are the sources of the *man-in-the-moon* legend. According to Brewer, the moon man is "leaning on a fork, on which he is carrying a bundle of sticks picked up on a Sunday." The *man in the moon* is a fancied semblance of a human face in the disk of the moon, so perceived because of the variations in the moon's topography. The moon man's intelligence must be questionable because this phrase is often preceded by "I know no more about it than. . . ."

moonshine illegally distilled whiskey; to distill or distribute liquor illegally, chiefly in rural areas of southeastern United States; empty or foolish talk. Despite its popularity in the United States, William and Mary Morris provide evidence that *moonshine* was used by the English to describe "illegally smuggled liquor by night" as early as the eighteenth century.

moonroof a transparent section of an auto roof that can be propped up, removed entirely, or remain fixed within the roof.

moonlight occurring by moonlight or at night; to work at an additional job after one's regular full-time employment, presumably at night.

blue moon a very long time. Brewer advises us that a *blue moon* was actually reported in a London paper on December 10, 1883. Modern meteorologists conclude that the blue appearance of the moon is caused by particles in the atmosphere that come from volcanos or forest fires.

moony dreamy, listless, or silly. A *Moony* can also be a member of a religious cult (the Unification Church) founded by Korean born Sun Myung Moon (1920–). This *Moony* has nothing to do with the orbital *moon*.

moonstruck mentally deranged, supposedly by the influence of the moon; crazed; dreamily romantic.

I have tried to get to the bottom of the quaint custom of *mooning*, exposing the buttocks usually at a window as a prank or as a gesture of disrespect, but have not as yet been successful.

Morocco/morocco

Morocco is a kingdom in northwest Africa bounded on the north by the Mediterranean Sea, on the southwest by the Spanish **Sahara,** on the east and south by Algeria, and on the west by the Atlantic Ocean. It is nine miles from Spain, separated by the Strait of Gibraltar. The Arab name for Morocco is *El Maghreb-el-aksa* which means the farthest west. Its name was anglicized to Morocco. Morocco is now a constitutional monarchy.

One of Morocco's principal exports is *Moroccan* leather, a fine, pebble-grained leather originally made in Morocco from goat skin tanned with sumac. This kind of leather was used as a binding for fine books and, accordingly, Morocco developed the sense of something imposing or proper—a solid Moroccan-bound tradition, for example. Moroccan leather has become a generic term for leather made in imitation of Moroccan leather.

Motown sound

The nickname of a placename can legitimately be classified as a toponym. I have included several in this book, for example, **The Big Apple.** *Motown* is a special case because, although it started out as a nickname of a nickname, it went on to develop a completely independent sense. *Motown* was and is a shortened version of Motor City, itself a nickname of Detroit, Michigan, an important automobile manufacturing center.

In 1959, Berry Gordy, Jr., borrowed $800 from his family savings account, according to *The Motown Story,* a book by Don Waller. He used the money to make a recording. While his first record was on the Tamla label, within months he was recording on the *Motown* label. His first gold record (a million copies sold) was "Shop Around" by the Miracles in 1961. The list of *Motown* recording artists includes such names as Diana Ross, Smokey Robinson, Stevie Wonder, Marvin Gaye, and the Jackson Five.

The place where it all started, 2648 West Grand Boulevard, Detroit, Michigan, is now a museum. Berry Gordy moved his Motown record company to the City of the Angels in 1972, but by that time *Motown* had taken on a new meaning apart from the Detroit city from whence it came. *The Motown sound* has come to describe an upbeat, style of rhythm and blues associated with the city of Detroit, and vocalists and groups since the 1950s, and characterized by danceable arrangements.

Motown seems to us to be anatopic (out of place) in Los Angeles. A more appropriate name for this sound might now be Tintown, a foreshortened version of Tinseltown.

Munich/Munich Pact

In *Safire's Political Dictionary*, the author makes the point that cities and even small towns have become toponyms as a result of an historic event or conference that occurred there. He cites Guernica, Sarajevo, and Yalta in that category. A quick check of my standard dictionaries revealed no new definitions, but only geographical and demographic information about those places. I shall give Mr. Safire the benefit of the doubt and assume that in political counsels such words do have currency, albeit esoteric. *Munich* is another matter. It is a legitimate toponym with its own special definition.

Munich (Munchen) is a city in and the capital of Bavaria, in southwest West Germany, with a population of 1.3 million. *Munich* is also cited as any dishonorable appeasement. This special definition stemmed from a pact signed in *Munich* by Great Britain, France, Italy, and Germany on September 29, 1938. At that meeting, the Sudetanland was ceded to Germany in order to appease Adolph Hitler. The English Prime Minister, Neville Chamberlain, returned to England after the signing to declare that they had achieved, "Peace in our time." The pact was a monumental error and Chamberlain's prediction of "peace" proved to be one of the greatest political miscalculations of all time. Twenty million people died during the "peace" (World War II) that followed.

NNNNNNNNNNN**N**NNNNNNNNNNN

Naugahyde

Naugatuck is a manufacturing town (population 26,500) in central Connecticut that achieved semitoponymy by having the first element of its Indian name incorporated into the synthetic, hard-wearing, leatherlike, and trademarked fabric, *Naugahyde,* first produced there in 1937. The word *Naugahyde* combines *Nauga,* the first element in Naugatuck, and *hyde* from hide, an animal skin. According to the *Oxford English Dictionary, Naugahyde* consists of a "fabric base coated with a layer of rubber or vinyl resin and finished with a grain like that of leather."

Like formica (used for countertops), *naugahyde* has often been used generically in its lower-cased form to describe all such simulated leather products. For example, in H. Nielsen's novel, *The Severed Key* (1973), it was used as follows: "The apartment was finished in contemporary motel *naugahyde.*" This special usage of *Naugahyde* suggests a sense of the ordinary. Imagine, if you will, what the name of the product might have been if it had been developed on Jekyll Island in the Atlantic Ocean off the coast of South Carolina. A monstrous thought!

Neanderthal/neanderthal

You are about to meet a long-lost ancestor. I am, of course, referring to the *Neanderthal man* who was discovered in the Neander Gorge near Dusseldorf, West Germany, in 1856. *Neander* is a placename of unknown origin, but the *-thal* suffix, usually attached to the word, has a few relations of its own—for example, *dale,* a valley; *dell* (as in farmer in the dell), a little valley; and a **dollar.**

This particular relative, *Neanderthal,* lived 35,000 to 100,000 years ago. He was about 5 feet 2 inches in height, had large brow ridges, walked erect, and had powerful teeth. The remains of this particular branch of the human family were found in at least 40 different archaeological digs in Europe, but the first one was found at the Neander site for which it was named. The *Neanderthals* were excellent hunters who followed the herds and lived in temporary shelters and caves.

Although the *Neanderthal* man is extinct, the *neanderthal* name continues to be used informally, today, to describe a person who is primitive, backward, reactionary, or just plain ignorant. Perhaps you know someone who fits this description.

Newcastle, carry (or send) coals to

Newcastle-on-Tyne, also called Newcastle, is an industrial city in the northeast of England that got its modern name from the construction of a new castle in the twelfth century. Its main claim to fame, later on, was the huge production of coal that was mined and shipped from there. The large coal trade inspired the *coals to Newcastle* idiom, which first appeared in print in 1662, and came to mean to take something to a place where it already exists in great quantity. It can also mean to do more than is required, ordered, or expected. The ancient Latin equivalent would be *aquam mari infundere,* meaning to pour water into the sea. The modern version of the *Newcastle* colloquialism could easily be to *carry cocaine to Colombia,* which certainly has the alliterative power, if not the BTU (British thermal units) energy, of the *carry coals to Newcastle* version.

New Yorkese

In *The Treasure of Our Tongue,* Lincoln Barnett suggests that, "The evolution of the name of York presents an example of English linguistic history in miniature." *York* is derived from a Celtic word, *Eburacon,* meaning the place of the yew trees. The Roman or Latin version of *Eburacon* was *Eburacus,* and *Novus Eburacus* appears on the official seals of the state and city of New York. The Anglo-Saxon invasion of Britain started about A.D. 450, and these Germanic tribes translated *Eburacus* as *Eoforic,* meaning boar town. Later, the Vikings translated *Eoforic* as *Iorvik.* In time, *Iorvik* became *Iork* and eventually *York.* In addition to the **New York minute,** there are several other New York typonymical terms of note:

New York steak/New York shell steak/New York strip/New York cut All of these terms are synonyms for a shell steak which is actually a porterhouse steak with the fillet removed. These names surfaced in 1970–1975. The porterhouse steak, which was named after Martin Morrison's Porter House (New York City) restaurant, founded in 1814, is a choice cut of beef from between the prime ribs and the sirloin.

New York School A loosely associated group of American and European artists and sculptors, especially abstract expressionist painters active in and near New York City in the 1940s and 1950s.

New York Curb Exchange This was the former name for the American Stock Exchange which first met on the curbs of New York City.

New Yorkese, the title of this section, is simply a speech or accent thought to be characteristic of New York City residents.

New York minute

I am indebted to William Safire for this toponymous idiom that appeared in his *On Language* column in the Sunday *New York Times.* Safire defines a *New York minute* as "instantly; without hesitation." The expression is one that is not heard around the New York City area, but is a reference used by citizens of U.S. southern states to the apparent fast pace of New Yorkers. The idiom has a derogatory ring to it, because southern people prefer a more relaxed pace than that of the New Yorkers they observe when visiting **The Big Apple.**

Safire further defines an even smaller moment in time, the *New York split second,* as "the time it takes for the light in front of you to turn green and the time the guy in back of you honks his horn." An interval that any New Yorker can verify to be very quick. A *California instant,* by the way, is the interval between the time you honk your horn at the car in front of you and the moment the driver gives you the California freeway signal (a crude gesture made with one's middle finger).

Nicene Creed

The *Nicene Creed* (also known as the Profession of Faith) used in the Roman Catholic and other Christian faiths, currently starts like this:

We believe in one God,
the Father, the Almighty,
maker of heaven and earth,
of all that is seen and unseen.

This Creed or prayer, which was a formal statement of the chief tenets of the Christian belief, was adopted at the first Council of Nicaea in A.D. 325. Nicaea was in northwest Turkey. It was the Emperor Constantine who called this special council that, in addition to adopting the Creed, established the time for observing Easter.

Nicaea was built by Antigonus Monophthalmus in 316 B.C. on a deserted site he called *Antigonia*. Soon afterward, Lysimachus changed its name from Antigonia to Nicaea, naming it after his wife. Today Nicaea is known in the west as Nice—the anglicized version of this placename.

OOOOOOOO**O**OOOOOOOO

Off Broadway. See **Broadway.**

OK

There are several explanations for the origin of *OK*, the international expression of affirmation which remains the most universally used of all words in any language.

Most accepted sources attribute *OK* to the nickname of a nineteenth century political club. *O and K* were the initials of Old Kinderhook, the nickname of Martin Van Buren's (president 1837–1841) birthplace, Kinderhook, New York. The *OK* letters appeared on the banners of the *OK* Club, the Democratic party's political organization in 1840. The nickname did not prove successful for Van Buren as the voters failed to elect him to a second term.

Within the last few years, *OK* has been voguishly used as a conversational crutch, a device to punctuate sentences and phrases. Personally, I deplore the use of *OK* in this way, *OK?*

Olympic Games/Olympiad/ Olympian

On the plains of Elis in the northwestern part of the Peloponnesus peninsula of Greece lies Olympia, an ancient religious center. It was here in 776 B.C. that the *Olympic Games* began. The discovery of these ruins so inspired a French educator, Baron Pierre de Coubertin, that he organized the first modern *Olympiad* in Athens in 1896, in which eight nations took part.

The *Olympic Games* were a combination patriotic, religious, and athletic festival. According to historical records, the first *Olympic* festival in 776 B.C. had only one contest, the 200-yard sprint. The games continued until A.D. 394 when the Roman emperor Theodosus banned the *Olympics,* because he held that they were pagan in nature. The nearly thousand-year history of this event was so ingrained in the minds of the Greeks that the word *Olympiad* had come to refer to a period of four years reckoned from the first ancient *Olympics* in 776 B.C. *Olympian,* to this day, can mean a contestant in the *Olympic Games.* And because of the exalted status of *Olympic* victors, *Olympian* also came to mean majestic in manner, superior to mundane affairs, or aloof.

While women were not permitted to attend the ancient games, the modern *Olympics* opened its doors to female participation in 1900.

ottoman

Instances in which a country or empire was named after a person are rare. One fairly modern example of this phenomenon is Saudi Arabia named after the founder of the present dynasty, Saudi ibn Abdul-Aziz (1901–1969). The Ottoman Empire is another case in point. It was founded in the thirteenth century by Othman or Osman (1299–1326) on the Asia Minor peninsula and lasted until after World War I when it was dismantled by the great powers (see **Balkanize**) who felt that the Ottoman Empire had outlived its usefulness. It achieved its greatest territorial expansion in the sixteenth century under Suleiman when the Empire included much of the Middle East and reached as far as Italy and encompassed most of North Africa.

There is, to be sure, ample evidence remaining of this once great empire including its architecture and art. At the bottom of this list is a family of seating appurtenances that took their name from the lower-case form, *ottoman*, to describe a cushioned couch, sofa, stool, or low cushioned seat without back or arms, that were either peculiar to the Ottoman period or inspired by it.

pppppppppppppPppppppppppppp

paisley/Paisley

The *paisley* print, currently so popular in men's ties and ladies' scarves and dress fabrics, had a definite westward pattern of exportation from its birthplace in Bukhara (see **buckra**) in the central Asian part of the Soviet Union. Now shawls made with similar patterns, though, are usually associated with **Cashmere** (Kashmir), now a part of India, where the most beautiful shawls were hand embroidered of cashmere wool. In 1798, the Cashmere version of the shawl was introduced into Europe where it became immensely popular as a protective or ornamental covering worn over the shoulder, neck, or head. The size of these outdoor garments were usually quite large and they were rectangular or triangular in shape.

The nineteenth century could be called the shawl (from the Persian word *shal*) period. In order to keep up with the demand for the Cashmeres, the weavers of Paisley, Renfrewshire, Scotland, urged on by the town's thread-manufacturing industry, set their hand looms to making less expensive copies of the Asian imports. The *Paisley* weavers created their own adaptation of the Cashmere patterns, rather than simply imitating them. As a result, the distinctive pattern of those Scottish weavers became known as *paisley*.

Paisley is now a generic word and the *paisley* pattern is produced all over the world. Perhaps this lovely pattern's popularity has something to do with the fact that the food stains that inevitably end up on a man's ties can not be easily detected on the intricately patterned *paisley* prints.

palace

In the fifteenth century, King Henry VIII of England started renovating the old castle fortresses that dotted the English countryside. By removing the three-inch archer's windows and other features that, at an earlier time, facilitated defense of the structures, these fortresses were transformed into *palaces*—large country homes suited to the nobility. It was the Romans, however, who gave us the word *palace*.

Augustus Caesar, the first emperor of Rome, had a home on the Palatium or Palatine Hill. The French converted *Palatium* to *palais*. But this word construction did not end here.

The etymological foundation for *palace* is the Latin word *palus*, a fenced enclosure used for grazing animals. A *palace*, therefore, was originally a pasture, which seems like as good a place as any to build a *palace*.

Paladin

For six years, starting in 1957, a T.V. show entitled *Have Gun Will Travel* was one of the most popular programs of its time. The part of Paladin, the central character of this 30-minute weekly western, was played by Richard Boone. In the show, Paladin traveled throughout the West as a hired gun available to anyone with a just cause or who was being victimized by more powerful forces. Paladin's calling card read "Have Gun Will Travel."

Originally, a *paladin* was any one of the 12 legendary peers or knightly champions in attendance on Charlemagne (742–814). This great king of the Franks and Romans was also known as *Carolus Magnum,* Charles the Great. As titles go, Charlemagne fared much better than his father who was known as Pepin the Short.

Paladin can be traced to the Latin word *palatinus,* a high-ranking official of a royal palace, and is ultimately traceable to the Palatine Hill in Rome from whence the word **palace** is derived. *Paladin* is used today to describe any knightly heroic champion or determined defender of a noble cause.

It is ironic that the producers of *HGWT* were sued for plagiarism by an arena performer who, it is said, looked like Boone, used the name Paladin, and had inscribed on his calling cards the words "Have Gun Will Travel." This twentieth-century *paladin* hired his own legal *paladins* who championed his cause and eventually obtained financial damages from those who sought to rob him of his identity.

Panama. See **Homburg.**

pandemonium

There are quite a few words, and several placenames too, that were created by the imaginations of literary authors. For example, **Lilliput, Shangri-la, Utopia,** and of course, *pandemonium,* a wild uproar or disorder; tumult or chaos. This word originally was coined by John Milton (1608–1674) and appeared in his 12-book epic poem entitled *Paradise Lost* (1667).

Pandemonium, like **Hades,** was actually the capital of hell in Milton's masterpiece, which was based on the story of creation and the fall of Satan and Adam and Eve. Milton himself was a deeply religious scholar who showed a rare literary ability as a youth and later at Christ College, Cambridge, England. Milton's own life was filled with *pandemonium* in 1649 when he was arrested for having held a government position during the Cromwell years. He was, however, not punished.

Paradise Lost was written during his retirement at a time when he was totally blind. Legend has it that he dictated the poem to his two daughters. *Pandemonium* combines Greek word elements that literally mean all demons. Being in a state of *pandemonium* can be a living hell for some, but others seem to thrive on disorder.

parchment

The residents of Pergamum, an ancient Greek city and kingdom (of the same name) covering most of the eastern part of Asia Minor (Turkey), discovered at a very early stage in history that necessity is the mother of invention. Having been deprived of papyrus by an Egyptian cartel, they developed *parchment*, a substitute material that adequately satisfied their need for a durable and highly portable writing surface. Unlike papyrus, *parchment* is still in use as a writing surface.

The R&D (Research and Development) of *parchment* was ordered by Eumenes II, King of Pergamum, in 190 B.C. The development of this substitute writing material, named for its place of origin, Pergamum, was a reaction to the reigning Egyptian pharoah's decree that no papyrus could be sold to Pergamum. The pharoah's embargo resulted from his fear that the library of Pergamum might exceed his own great library in Alexandria, Egypt.

Parchment is produced from the skins of sheep, goats, and other animals. They would first remove the hairs from the skins and then place the skins in lime to remove the fat. They were then stretched on frames and shaved with knives and scrapers. Next, powdered chalk was rubbed on with pumice stones. This softened the skin and created a smooth writing surface. The finest *parchment* is called *vellum* and is made of calf, kid, and lamb skins. *Parchment* is still used for some diplomas, and as a result we often refer to such documents as "sheepskins."

The development of *parchment* was an excellent solution to the papyrus embargo, but I suspect that the goats and sheep were not crazy about it.

Parnassus

Mount Parnassus was so important in ancient Greek mythology that its name has survived to grace modern English even though the mountain is no longer called Parnassus but Liakoura. Despite the name change, the mountain's location remains north of the Gulf of Corinth in Greece, directly behind and above Delphi (see **Delphic Oracle**). In ancient times, Mt. Parnassus was sacred to Apollo, the god of the sun, music, poetry, and art, among other things. He was also considered to be the best looking of all the gods in the Greek pantheon.

The early Apollo-Parnassus connection can be observed in the present-day phrase, *ascent to Parnassus*, which suggests that a person is going into art, particularly poetry or music. *Parnassus* can also be a collection of poems or elegant literature, the world of poetry, any center of poetry or artistic endeavor, or a specific reference to a French school of poetry.

parting shot/Parthian shot

Parthia was an ancient country that geographically coincides with modern-day Khorasan, a province in northeast Iran. In their earlier history (500 B.C.), the Parthians were pushovers, militarily speaking, as their armies were defeated by a series of great generals including Cyrus the Great of Persia and Alexander the Great of Macedonia. However, their fortunes took an aboutface when they discovered that turnabout was not only fair play, but smart tactics as well. In 53 B.C. the Parthians defeated the Roman general Crassus with a unique new maneuver they had perfected. Again, in 36 B.C. they defeated another general, Mark Anthony, with this same tactic. Great military victories turn on such strategies.

Parthian mounted archers were noted for their unique military skills. They specialized in racing at their enemies while firing arrows (or darts). They would then suddenly turn about, as if in retreat, and continue firing missile after missile backwards at the enemy. This strategy required great skill and was extremely successful. The technique, known as a *Parthian shot*, has survived as an idiom, but is usually expressed as a *parting shot*. Both idioms are defined as a threat, insult, retort, or the like, uttered on leaving. *Parting shots* are most difficult to respond to, because by the time the target of such a verbal missile can respond, the one delivering the sarcastic dart has disappeared.

Pekin/Pekingese/Peking Man/ Peking duck

Beijing is the capital of The People's Republic of China, but it also became a symbol of oppression when the Chinese government brutally crushed the student's outcry for greater democracy there in June of 1989. Before its spelling and pronunciation were changed, Beijing was known over the past several centuries as *Peking, Peiching,* and *Peiping*. *Peking* combines two Chinese language elements, *Pe-*, north, and *-king*, capital. In this older form, the ancient city of Peking has several more favorable associations, including:

Pekin A silk fabric in which broad stripes of equal width and in various colors or weaves are alternated.

Pekingese A Chinese breed of dog having a long, silky coat, usually brown in color, or a native of Peking, or the standard Chinese language.

Peking man A prehistoric man who lived 375,000 years ago in what is now northeastern China. This man, *homo erectus Pekinensis*, was first found in the 1920s, but his remains were lost in 1941 when they were shipped from China for safekeeping.

Peking duck A specialty of Chinese cooking prized for its crisp skin. It is prepared by forcing air between the meat and skin, brushing it with water, and hanging it up to dry before cooking.

pell-mell. See mall.

Peoria, play in/Peoria soup

Public response to a national political campaign is extremely important to those who make a living out of politics. But why should the reaction of the Peorians be of greater concern than other places? I shall explain the reasons and hope that it *plays in Peoria,* a fine city in central Illinois.

In 1968, John Erhlichman, a former Nixon White House aide and convicted Watergate conspirator, coined the *Peoria* phrase which has come to mean how it will be received outside of Washington in a less politically sophisticated area. He probably used *Peoria* for no other reason than the fact that in his mind it was synonymous with Mainstream America or Middle America. The alliterative combination of *play* and *Peoria* probably created more appeal than, perhaps, "play in Springfield" might have produced. The idiom is apparently based on the theater sense of a play's ability to succeed in certain regional theaters.

Peoria soup, which is a very thin soup made by boiling lots of water with a few scraps of meat and vegetables thrown in, is an example of folk (false) etymology. According to Chapman, the Peoria in this thin soup is based on the mispronunciation of *puree*. The idiom can be traced back to hobo use in the 1920s.

Persian. See **Karacul.**

Philadelphia lawyer

"If you are innocent, trust in God; If you are guilty, get a *Philadelphia lawyer*." This satirical bit of wisdom suggests that *Philadelphia lawyers* are a particularly clever lot. Let us trace the origin of this special idiom which refers to a shrewd lawyer adept at the discovery and manipulation of legal technicalities.

Peter Zenger (1697–1746), a German-born printer living in New York City, published articles exposing corruption by the English Colonial Governor. To defend a libel suit brought against him, Zenger, in desperation, petitioned Andrew Hamilton, a retired *Philadelphia lawyer*, to assist him. Hamilton responded to Zenger's urgent plea for help and successfully defended him, and, moreover, would not accept a fee for doing so.

This precedent-setting case firmly established the right to freedom of speech in the colonies, and was later preserved for all time in the First Amendment to the Bill of Rights.

Philistine/philistine

The *Philistines* were initially members of an Aegean people who lived on Crete and other islands that are now a part of Greece.

They were driven out of their homelands by northern tribes in the twelfth century B.C. After plundering several eastern Mediterranean towns, they finally settled in Canaan, an area that is now roughly equivalent to the Gaza Strip. The Greeks called this area *Philistia,* a word that via Latin and Hebrew was eventually rendered to *Palestine.* After centuries of harassing the Israelites, the *Philistines* were finally assimilated by them.

The *Philistines* were never totally accepted by the Israelites who considered them to be somewhat barbaric and unenlightened. This sense surfaced again in the nineteenth century as *philistine* became lower cased and defined as a person lacking in or hostile to cultural values, aesthetics, refinements, or who is commonplace in ideas and tastes. It is ironic that, although the Israelites looked down upon the *Philistines,* a version of that word, *Palestine,* was ultimately adopted by them as the name of their country in Biblical times.

piker

There is enough evidence to attest to the probability that *piker,* one who does things in a small or petty way, came from Pike County, Missouri. The *Random House Dictionary,* however, indicates that *piker* probably comes from a Middle English word meaning a petty thief.

Digging further, I find that Eric Partridge suggests that *piker* is a slang version of *picayune,* a New Orleans French five-cent piece, which came to mean something of slight value. As so often happens in word development, especially the development of slang words, similar words independently developed often end up reinforcing each other. On this one you have a peck of *pikers* to pick from, but my pick is the toponymous Pike County etymology.

podunk/Podunk

According to the *Oxford English Dictionary*, a 1933 magazine article established *Podunk* as a jocular generic term for insignificant and backward small towns or colleges in the United States. Here is a quote from that piece: "It (the 18th Amendment) required one rule for Podunk, Kansas, and one for New York City." Is there actually a place by the name of *Podunk?* If so, where is it? What is the origin of the name *Podunk?* And, finally, is a college or university located there?

There are actually two places named *Podunk,* neither of which is in Kansas. One is the hamlet of *Podunk,* Massachusetts, near Worcester. There is also a *Podunk* in Connecticut on the *Podunk* River in Hartford County. The name *Podunk* is of Algonquin Indian origin and simply means a pocket or neck of land. To the best of my knowledge, there is no college or university by that name.

polka/polka dot/polonaise

Freedom, and even the prospect of freedom, is certainly something to dance about. The people of Prague, Czechoslovakia, it is said, adopted a popular folk dance of Bohemia (see **bohemian**), called the *polka,* in tribute to the unsuccessful Polish rebellion against the Russians in 1830. The word *polka,* while meaning Polish woman in the Polish language, is more likely derived from the Czech word *pulka,* meaning a half step. The pulka word for the dance was eventually reshaped to *polka.* Just as Polka means Polish woman, the word *Polak,* before it became an offensive ethnic slur, meant Polish person in the language of the Poles.

The *polka* dance was a huge success and quickly spread to other European countries and to America. Manufacturers began adopting the name of the dance as a trademark for articles of clothing, food, and ornaments. An American dressmaker produced a fabric in the 1880s which had a pattern of uniform and equidistant dots. The fabric was called *polka dot* in homage to the popular *polka dance.* There is no apparent connection between the *polka dot* fabric and the dance itself.

The *polka's* identification with Poland may be just another case of folk (false) etymology or simply mistaken identity. The *polonaise,* however, is another matter. *Polonaise,* meaning Polish dance, also may have been inspired by the *polka.* In 1989, the Poles and Czechs had something to kick up their heels about once again as democracy has replaced communist oppression in those countries. Perhaps these events will inspire a new dance.

polonaise. See **polka.**

pompadour

King Louis XV of France (1710–1774) was married to Marie Leszczynska of Poland in 1725 at the age of 15. He had nine children with Marie, but still found time for a few royal mistresses including the Marquise de Pompadour (1721–1764). While Louis' reign was undistinguished, Madame de Pompadour had an illustrious career as a fashion trendsetter. Unlike Louis XV, her name has been immortalized in the English language by a hairdo that she apparently wore and that bears her name, the *pompadour.* The *pompadour* is a coiffure in which the hair is brushed up high above the forehead.

Madame de Pompadour was born Jeanne Antoinette Poisson, a middle-class woman who had been well educated. In 1741 she was married to Lenormand d'Etoiles and became socially prominent in Paris even before she caught Louis' eye and became his official mistress. Louis made her the marquise of the obscure marquisate of Pompadour, a locality in Correge, an area of south central France. It is of minor historical interest that Louis' famous great grandfather, Louis XIV, the Sun King, also had a famous mistress, Louise de LaValliere. Her name was immortalized in the word **lavalliere,** an ornament worn around the neck and more recently used as the name of a small television lapel microphone. Therefore, in the area of English word creation, the score is royal mistresses—2; kings—0.

port. See **sherry.**

portland cement

The Egyptians were using a gypsum (from the Arab word *jibs,* meaning mortar) plaster as mortar in the construction of the pyramids 4,500 years ago. But the credit for making water-resistant mortar goes to the Greeks and Romans who made a pozzolana mortar by mixing finely ground volcanic material with lime, sand, and water. *Pozzolana* is derived from the Italian town of Pozzuoli where volcanic material could be found. This kind of cement was used to build the Pantheon (which is still standing and very much in use) and the Coliseum, both in Rome. Although this early cement had great durability, it fell into disuse with the fall of the Roman Empire in the fourth century A.D. It was not until the eighteenth century that the English began experimenting with the manufacture of cement once again.

In 1824 Joseph Apsdin, a British bricklayer, invented and patented a cement which he named *portland.* His cement was superior to others available at the time and was made by mixing, grinding, burning, and regrinding limestone and clay. He chose the name *portland* because of his cement's resemblance to Portland stone, a limestone quarried on the Isle of Portland, Dorsetshire, England.

The first *portland cement* plant in the United States was established in 1871. By 1898, there were some 91 different formulas. The composition of *portland cement* was not standardized until 1917 after the establishment of the Portland Cement Association in 1916. There you have *the whole nine yards* (an idiom that comes from the fact that concrete trucks at one time held nine yards of concrete) on the origin of Portland cement.

Potemkin village

On a 1989 trip to Leningrad our Russian guide introduced me to the *Potemkin village* expression and its interesting origin. *Potemkin village,* like a Hollywood set, is not a real village, but a Russian colloquialism that immortalized the betrayal of Empress Catherine II by Grigori Potemkin. Potemkin, according to historians, was the first of Catherine the Great's (1729–1796) many lovers. He was also a mediocre general and Catherine's longtime advisor and correspondent. Later, as governor of the Crimea, he was entrusted with funds that were to be used to improve the poor conditions in the villages. Instead, Potemkin diverted the money to his personal use.

During Catherine's tour of the Crimea in 1787, Potemkin deceived her by building sham villages of cardboard to hide the area's actual poverty. Potemkin's duplicity was eventually discovered, and he ended up out in the cold, banished by Catherine to Siberia. A *Potemkin village* is defined as a pretentiously showy or impossible facade intended to mask or divert attention from an embarrassing or shabby fact or condition. The beautifully restored monuments of the Soviet Union, such as its cathedrals, the Hermitage, and the many restored palaces and buildings provide a modern equivalent to the *Potemkin village;* such restorations masked the true condition of the failing Soviet economy and the poor state of the Russian people.

Potomac fever/Potomac phosphate/ All quiet on the Potomac

The Greek word for river is *potamios.* Despite the similarity between *Potomac* and *potamios,* there is no connection between the two. Some historians, however, cite these two words as proof that the ancient Greeks had a pre-Columbian (or pre-Ericson) settlement in North America. Our *Potomac* potpourri includes these idioms:

Potomac fever the determination or fever that grips otherwise sensible people who want to share the power or prestige of the U.S. government in Washington, D.C., by being elected or appointed to a government position.

Potomac phosphate a jocular local synonym for drinking water similar to the Hudson (River) or Croton (Reservoir) cocktail—both are also nicknames for water.

All quiet on the Potomac peaceful; undisturbed; a time of ease or quiet enjoyment. This phrase is attributed to its frequent use in General George B. McClellan's bulletins issued during the Civil War.

Punic faith/Punic treachery/ Punic art/Punic deceit

Nationalistic fervor has resulted in a number of international epithets. These epithets serve as verbal missiles in the often ageless hostilities between nations. For instance, England referred to "false" courage obtained from drinking whiskey as **Dutch courage.** The Italians and English referred to syphilis as the **French disease.** (This disease was actually named after the French even before it became known as syphilis). Another set of slurs, and the focal point of this discussion, are the Punic idioms—*fides, perfida, ars,* and *fraus Punica.* All four epithets charge the Phoenicians with treachery and deceit and were attributed to the Carthaginians by the Romans.

Punic is derived from *Punicas,* the Latin word for the Phoenicians, a Semitic tribe that waged a triad of wars against the Romans for supremacy in the Mediterranean. The so-called Punic Wars were waged between Carthage, the Phoenician city-state on the northern coast of Africa, and Rome (264–146 B.C.) The Romans won all three, after which they razed Carthage. *Phoenician* (Punicus) is thought by some to be derived from a Greek word meaning blood-red or purple. Perhaps they were so called because of the purple and scarlet robes worn by Phoenician noblemen.

The Phoenicians are not only remembered for the Punic insults coined by their Roman enemies, but more importantly for the development of the alphabet. It is ironic that the Phoenician alphabet, which was passed on to the Romans by the Greeks, was an important communication tool used by the Romans to build their empire. The Phoenician's own invention, therefore, came full circle to eventually aid in their downfall.

QQQQQQQQQQQQQQQQQQ

Queensbury rules

The Marquisate of Queensberry began with Scotsman William Douglas in 1640, but it was not until the time of the Ninth Marquis of Queensberry, alias Sir John Sholto Douglas (1844–1900), that a Queensberry stepped into the boxing ring and made it a square deal for participants. Before Sir John, boxing had been a chaotic and brutal spectacle going back to the Sumerians some five thousand years ago. Three thousand years later the Romans, who fought with a leather glove (cestus) on each fist, outlawed boxing. But in England of the 1800s boxing had reverted to the bare-knuckle affair that it had been in ancient Sumeria.

All that changed when the Ninth Marquis of Queensberry, a boxing enthusiast, helped to establish the London Prize Ring Rules in 1867. The three-minute round, the one-minute rest period between rounds, and the ten-second count for knockouts, rules that were initiated by Queensberry, are still in use today. It wasn't until 1872, however, that gloves were once again introduced to the sport. The very last professional bare-knuckle boxing match took place in 1889, when John L. Sullivan *took off the gloves* and defeated Jack Kilrain. And those are the bare facts.

Quonset (quonset) hut

In 1941, at the outset of World War II, a temporary shelter was first built at Quonset Point Naval Air Station, Rhode Island. The advantage of this semicylindrical corrugated metal hut was that it could be prefabricated and shipped to U.S. bases anywhere in the world and quickly assembled. They were usually 50 or 100 feet long and 20 to 40 feet high, depending on their length. These structures were used as barracks or for storage.

The American name for this particular shelter, *Quonset,* was taken from the place where it was first made and the word is now trademarked. The British call their version of the *Quonset* a British Nissen Hut, and while it may sound suspiciously as if it were manufactured by the Japanese, it was actually named for its original designer, British Colonel P. N. Nissen. *Quonset,* incidentally, comes from the Indian word *Seconquonset* (land jutting into the water); in fact, the *quonset hut* looks very much like the Iroquois Indian long houses.

RRRRRRRRRRR**R**RRRRRRRRRRR

rhinestone

The Rhine River that flows past Strasbourg, Germany, was the source of the *rhine* in *rhinestone. Rhinestones* were originally a variety of rock crystal from the Rhine River area. The French called them *caillon du Rhin*, literally pebble of the Rhine. Later, in the 1880s, a colorless artificial gem of paste and strass, cut to resemble a diamond, was developed in Strasbourg and called *rhinestone*.

Strass, incidentally, was a hard glass with a high lead content used to imitate gemstones. It was named after its German inventor, J. Strasser. And there you have the complete story of the *rhinestone* except for its recent idiomatic usage. For example, the *rhinestone* in the movie *Rhinestone Cowboy* suggests an imitation or fake cowboy.

rhubarb

In order to prevent a *rhubarb* over whether *rhubarb* is a vegetable or a fruit, I shall settle this issue at the outset. *Rhubarb* is a vegetable! However, it is usually prepared as a dessert food, often as pie filling and sweet sauces and, therefore, many people assume that it is a fruit.

Rhubarb is defined as several plants belonging to the genus Rheum of the buckwheat family. The name of this vegetable that tastes like fruit is derived from the Latin word *rhabarbarum*. Its prefix, *rha-*, was derived from the ancient name, Rha, for the Volga River, the longest river in Europe, where this plant grew profusely. The *-barb* element is obtained from the Latin *barbarum* (see **barbarian**) meaning foreign. *Rhabarbarum* was literally the fruit from the Rha or Volga.

Some experts conclude that *rhubarb,* used in the first sentence of this piece and meaning a quarrel or dispute, is theatrical slang dating back to the days of Shakespeare. *Rhubarb* is the word repeated by actors and extras to this day to simulate the sound of a quarrelsome crowd. The word eventually was transferred to mean the quarrel or dispute itself.

rialto

We have a movie theater in our town named the Rialto, which I suspect is a fairly common name for such theaters. *Rialto* is defined as a theater and market district originally named after an island in Venice on which a marketplace and theaters were situated. The island was on the Grand Canal and was connected to San Marco Island by the Rialto Bridge, which was built in 1590. In time, a double row of shops was built on top of this very popular bridge. *Rialto* is an alteration of the Latin *rivus altus,* deep river.

According to Wilfred Funk, *rialto* was the name given to a New York City theatrical district that ran from Broadway to Fourth Avenue on 14th Street. This theater district moved uptown and is currently referred to as Broadway, or The Great White Way.

(*Rialto,* by the way, is not the only word that came from a

Venetian island and floated into the English language. The word **ghetto** was derived from another Venetian island.)

Roman numerals. See **Arabic and Roman numerals.**

Romance/romance/ romanesque

Roman males are not necessarily more given to, or expert at, *romance* than other men, although many female tourists who visit the Eternal City have complained (or boasted) that Roman men can be quite amorous in a pinch. My purpose here is not to get to the bottom of the curious customs of Roman males, however, but to explain the development of the featured Roman derivatives.

The *Romance* languages are so called because they are descended from the classic Latin language of the Romans. They include French, Provençal, Italian, Spanish and Portuguese, Romanian, Catalan, Rhaeto-Romanic, Sardinian, and Ladino. These hybrid languages developed when the Romans sent colonists to settle newly conquered possessions. The Roman soldiers, tradesmen, and farmers took their language with them; however, it was not the classic Latin, but the vulgar or popular Latin used in the everyday conversations of the common people. These colonists borrowed words from the conquered people, and the combination resulted in the distinct new languages listed above. Later, the Latin phrase *Romance scribere* was used to mean to write in the vernacular, instead of literary Latin. This expression eventually was shortened to *Romance* to describe these new crossbreed languages.

Romance was also applied to a long work of fiction that was less realistic than a novel. In ancient Greece, love stories were called *romances,* while war stories were called *epics.* From this sense, *romance* developed its current meaning of love affair, but is also used to mean fanciful and exaggerated. *Romanesque* is an English word borrowed from modern French and means fanciful and romantic.

Rosetta stone

One of the greatest archaeological discoveries of all time was the unearthing of the *Rosetta stone* by a French soldier in 1799. This great finding occurred during Napoleon Bonaparte's Egyptian military expedition. The *stone,* measuring 3 feet 9 inches in height and 2 feet 4 inches in width, is made of basalt (a very hard lava stone). It was found on a bank at the mouth of the Nile River near Rosetta, a town in northern Egypt. The slab, which was named for the place where it was uncovered, helped Egyptologists to unlock the mystery of the Egyptian Hieroglyphic language. It also helped unearth the history, customs, and religious beliefs of the ancient Egyptian civilization when these pictographs were later deciphered by Champolion, a French scholar.

The inscriptions neatly incised into the hard surface of the stone told of the coronation of Ptolemy V (203–181 B.C.). But instead of merely inscribing the message in one language, it was written in three languages, two of which were commonly used by the Egyptians at that time. From top to bottom the languages were: *hieroglyphics,* a Greek word meaning sacred writing; *demotic,* also a Greek word defined as popular language—of the people; and Greek, which is essentially the same today as it was in the time of Ptolemy V. The *Rosetta stone* also has become an idiom for a clue, breakthrough, or discovery that provides crucial knowledge for the solving of a puzzle.

Rubicon, cross the

Julius Caesar crossed many bodies of water during his conquest of Gaul, Britain, and even the Isle of Jersey (to which he gave his name). However, no crossing was more momentous than his *crossing (of) the Rubicon* in 49 B.C. This bold and historically important act was immortalized in the *Rubicon* phrase that means to take a final irrevocable step.

The Rubicon River marked the boundary between Roman Italy and Gaul. Roman generals were forbidden by law and tradition from marching their troops south of that borderline. Such an action was considered to be a threat to the security of the Roman rulers. This was an all-or-nothing gamble by the great Roman leader. Both Plutarch and Suetonus reported that before the crossing Caesar said, *"Iacta alea est,"* a common phrase of the day meaning the die is cast or an irrevocable decision has been made.

As his troops progressed through town after town on their way to Rome, they encountered little resistance, but were met instead by crowds of cheering citizens. By the time he reached Rome, Caesar's enemies, Pompey and his cohorts, were in full retreat. Caesar's all-or-nothing gamble paid off for him. You may want to *cross a Rubicon* yourself someday, but consider it carefully because you may be *ut fata trahunt* (at the mercy of destiny) when you do.

Rugby/rugby/rugger

In 1823, a young student by the name of William W. Ellis literally took the ball and ran with it. His singular action in many games, including the game of life, would have been applauded except for the fact that the game in which he was playing on that day, football (soccer), such an action was strictly forbidden. Ellis' historical run was prompted either by exuberance or frustration, but it caused his team such embarrassment that his captain was compelled to apologize profusely to the other team. All of this occurred at an English prep school, the Rugby School, in the city of Rugby in Warwickshire, central England.

Rugby, which is played between two teams with 15 members each, differs from soccer in the freedom to carry the ball, block with the hands and arms, and tackle. Rugby is also played with a different ball. It involves continuous action and no substitutions. The first element in the word *Rugby* is probably derived from a person named *Hrocai,* while the *-by* ending is derived from an Old Norse word *byr,* a farm or village. *Rugby* was not only the forerunner of American football, but it also inspired the *rugby* shirt, a fashion adapted from the style of shirt traditionally worn by *ruggers.*

On that historic day in 1823, one young man's shocking action caused him to be an island of contempt in the eyes of his peers (sort of an "Ellis Island"). But some of his teammates liked the idea of running with the ball and "had a ball" doing so. New ideas in art, science, and other endeavors often shock the establishment, but such radical actions by a very few are frequently the source of brilliant new achievements. Such was the case with *rugby,* which eventually led to the development of American football, much to the dismay of many a football widow during the football season.

runcible spoon

In Edward Lear's 1871 child's classic, *The Owl and the Pussycat,* there is this line:

> They dined on mince and slices of quince,
> which they ate with a *runcible spoon;*

Upon reading this, I was driven to discover the meaning and origin of this intriguing utensil, which I shall spoon feed to you now. The *Random House Dictionary* defines *runcible spoon* as "a forklike utensil with two broad prongs and one sharp, curved prong, as used in serving *hors d'oeurves.*" The word was coined by Edward Lear who is generally credited with the popularity of the **limerick.**

The word *runcible* was patterned on Roncevaux Pass (Ronces Valles) in the Spanish Pyrenees, where in A.D. 778 Charlemagne's army, under the command of Roland, was slaughtered by the Saracens. According to the *Oxford English Dictionary*, *runcible* was fashioned in jocose allusion to the slaughter at this famous battle and because of the sharp cutting edge on this *foonlike spork*. (Whoops! That should have read *spoonlike fork*, but I could not pass up this runcible *spoonerism* named after the Reverend William Archibald Spooner, the dean and later warden of New College, Oxford. Spooner, who lived to the ripe age of 86, suffered a speech affliction called metathesis, the accidental transposition of letters or syllables in the words of a sentence. Among the many accidental *spoonerisms* attributed to the Reverend are "We all know what it is, to have a half-warmed fish inside us," meaning to say "a half-formed wish"; he once explained to listeners that "the Lord is a shoving leopard"; and he once called Queen Victoria "our queer old dean" instead of "our dear old queen.")

Ruritania/Ruritanian

There are a great many toponyms that have been created by the stroke of a writer's pen (see **Utopia, Lilliput, Pandemonium,** and **Shangri-la.**) *Ruritania* is another placename that sprung from the pen (or typewriter, in which case we might call it a typonym). *Ruritania* was a fictional kingdom in central Europe created by Anthony Hope Hawkins (1863–1933), who wrote under the name A. Hope. Hope, an Englishman, wrote 32 novels and 2 dramas including *The Prisoner of Zenda* (1894), in which *Ruritania* first appeared. The author was trained as a lawyer, but abandoned the bar after the success of *Zenda*.

Ruritania has developed the facetious sense of any small, little-known country or region considered remote, backward, or exotic. Hope, according to noted etymologist Eric Partridge, fashioned his mythical fairyland country by combining the Latin word *ruralis*, meaning country, with a common placename ending, *-ania* (Pennsylv*ania*, Transylv*ania*). The adjectival form, *Ruritanian*, is still used to describe something that is characteristic of an imaginary kingdom or land. The model for *Ruritania* may have been the tiny country (population 19,000) of Liechtenstein.

Russian roulette

Battle-weary soldiers often adopted a fatalistic attitude toward life and so it is understandable that officers in the Russian Army fighting in World War I could have invented a deadly game of chance that came to be known as *Russian roulette*. In this dangerous pastime, a foolish person places a single bullet in a six-shooter (a revolver with six chambers). He then spins the cylinder, aims the gun at his head, and pulls the trigger. There is a one-in-six chance that the bullet will be in firing position and will mortally wound the player. Large sums of money were often wagered on this all-or-nothing gamble. Instead of going for broke, an unlucky participant went for kaput.

Russian roulette has developed the less sinister idiomatic sense of any foolhardy activity that may have a dangerous, if not deadly, result.

SSSSSSSSSSSSS**S**SSSSSSSSSSSSS

Sahara

Much to my surprise, a recent *New York Times Travel* article was entitled "Colorado's Sahara Sands." Since I was fairly certain that the real *Sahara* was in North Africa, and not Colorado, I grabbed my geographical dictionary to check on the true location of this gritty word, *Sahara*. Was the *Times* writer's use of *Sahara* correct in this instance? Would I be *plowing the sands*, an expression that means to employ fruitless labor, in order to find out about these sands of the *Times?*

I found, as expected, that the *real McCoy*, meaning the genuine article, in this case the *Sahara*, is in North Africa. It stretches from the Atlantic Ocean to the Nile Valley of Egypt and covers about 3.5 million square miles. I also discovered that the word *Sahara* is an Arabic word that literally means desert. Therefore, to refer to this desert as the *Sahara* desert is redundant, because it literally means desert desert.

Colorado's *Sahara*, which is officially known as Great Dunes National Monument, covers 55 square miles and goes from 100 feet below sea level to a height of 11,000 feet above. I also found that the word *Sahara* can be used to describe any wasteland. Therefore, the writer's use of *Sahara* in *The New York Times* article was absolutely correct.

San Quentin quail

Saint Quentin was a third-century martyr who has undoubtedly done a few revolutions in his grave upon discovering that his name has been memorialized by a state penitentiary in California. Gaius Quintinius, his Latin name, would be doubly disappointed to learn that a certain variety of young female game bird, much sought after by salacious predatory males, was also named after him. I am referring to the *San Quentin quail* species, defined as a girl below the legal age of sexual consent (the legal age of sexual consent in most states is 16 years), also referred to as jail bait. The use of San Quentin in this idiom, in lieu of the many other available prisons, is probably due to the alliterative or reduplicative force of the phrase.

The *quail* is a migratory game bird of Dutch origin and is akin to *quack.* According to Chapman, as early as the nineteenth century, *quail* was used as a college slang word for an attractive young woman; a chick. A pretty young woman today would more likely be called a fox, as the bird metaphors are on the wing. The San Quentin variety of quail, which first alighted in 1975–1980, survives as a euphemism for a pretty young girl (under 16 years of age), whose sexual favors can cost a man his freedom.

sardonic

There was a best-selling book published 20 or so years ago entitled *Please Don't Eat the Daisies* by Jean Kerr. I have no idea as to the toxicity of daisies, but I do know that there are many plants that are poisonous in varying degrees. For instance, in Sardinia there is a plant native to that island that is deadly poisonous and about which generations of anxious parents have warned their children. I have tracked down the name of this plant and the word inspired by its highly toxic action, *sardonic,* referring to a person who is scornfully mocking, derisive, or bitter.

The word *sardonic* actually stems from a highly poisonous plant known as *Herba Sardonia*. When taken internally, the herb twists its victim's face with a convulsive grin before causing certain death. Incidentally, the waters around Sardinia have also spawned schools of small fish known as *sardines*.

Scotch/Scotch whisky/scotch/ scot-free/Scotch Tape

About A.D. 500, a Celtic tribe from Ireland called the Scots invaded the land now called Scotland. The word *Scot* is from the Gaelic word *squit* meaning a wanderer. This bit of ethnic history explains why the Scottish and Irish both wear kilts and play the bagpipes. Here is an etymological key to the origins of several interesting words or phrases, related or not, that include a little drop of scotch (Scotch) in them:

Scotch of course, refers to the people of Scotland, but is also used in a derogatory way to describe a person who is tight with his or her money, or frugal.

Scotch whisky is a whiskey distilled in Scotland made from malted (grain that has been allowed to sprout) barley. Irish whiskey (with an "e") is its English, U.S., and Irish counterpart. I have never received a satisfactory explanation for why whiskey is spelled with an "e" in England, Ireland, and the U.S.A., while in Scotland and Canada it is spelled without an "e."

scotch means to make harmless, but does not come from the previous Scotch source. The source of this scotch is the Anglo-Norman word *escocher*, to notch.

scot-free simply means tax free. The *scot* in this idiom comes from a Middle English word of the same spelling and means tax.

Scotch Tape is a trademark of the 3M Company. It was originally developed as a tape for masking paint applications on two-tone automobiles. The tape was first made with adhesive on the edges only, and as a result the workers nicknamed the tape Scotch tape because they thought it was made that way to save on adhesive. The name Scotch tape stuck, and stuck, and stuck. . . .

Scotland Yard

Fiction writers have made *Scotland Yard* agents the heroes of many thrilling detective tales. My mission is to solve the mystery of how *Scotland Yard,* the pet name for the London Metropolitan Police, got its intriguing name.

During the reign of King Edgar of England (959–975), a gift of London real estate was bestowed upon King Kenneth of Scotland by the English monarch. Thereafter, Scottish kings were required to make an annual pilgrimage to London to pay homage to the English rulers. The site of the London residence of the highland kings was nicknamed *Scotland.*

The etymological evidence connecting the police with this piece of land is, as Sherlock Holmes would say, elementary. The link between the two was the location of the first English police force established in 1829, which was housed at 4 Whitehall Place, London. The entrance to this first headquarters building was from the *yard* formerly owned by the Scots and still called Scotland by Londoners of that day.

From the very beginning, the London Metropolitan Police Force was nicknamed *Scotland Yard,* and it is known by that name to this day, despite many moves from the original *Yard.*

Scylla and Charybdis, between

Sometimes we find ourselves *between a rock and a hard place*, or *on the horns of a dilemma*. These two modern idioms have their ancient equivalent (if not their actual origins) in *between Scylla and Charybdis* (pronounced *SIL*-ah and Ka-*RIB*-dis), meaning to be between two perils. This last metaphor remains in use today and is a favorite of etymologists.

Scylla (modern Scilla) was, and is still, a dangerous rock formation in the Straits of Messina, which divide Italy from Sicily. *Scylla* was on the Italian side. Of equal danger was a whirlpool known as *Charybdis* on the Sicilian side. The current between these twin terrors was very swift, and often a sea captain, while trying to steer clear of one of these two dangers, would drift into, and be destroyed by, the other. Greek mythologists, including Homer, personified these geographical phenomenon as sea monsters.

The best advice to sailors, of yesterday and today, when faced with such a dilemma is to steer a course right down the middle of these two perils, or just stay clear of them altogether.

seltzer

This sparkling etymology answers the questions, "What is the difference between *soda* and *seltzer*, and which came first?" The answers are that the two words are essentially synonymous, and *seltzer water* preceded *soda water* by four decades. *Seltzer* is an alteration of Selters, a village in Hesse-Nassau, Prussia (Germany). It was there that a naturally effervescent mineral water was found in the mid-eighteenth century. It had a high content of sodium, calcium, and magnesium carbonates as well as sodium chloride. The name for this sparkling water first appeared in print as *Selters water*, which was ultimately anglicized and lower-cased to *seltzer*.

The famed English scientist, Joseph Priestly (1733–1804), was the first to make an artificial soda water to imitate the water of Selters and other mineral springs. Today, *seltzer* and *soda* are interchangeable and are defined as water that has been commercially filtered, carbonated, and bottled with minerals or mineral salts. The word *seltzer* is still used regionally, but whether you prefer the word *soda* or *seltzer,* carbonated water remains very popular when mixed in hard or soft drinks.

serendipity

A Persian fairy tale retold in Horace Walpole's (1717–1797) *The Princes of Serendip* provided the English language with a new word, *serendipity,* the faculty of making fortunate and unexpected discoveries by accident. Such was the good fortune of the three princes of Serendip in Walpole's tale. Walpole, an Englishman, was an MP (Member of Parliament), author, and the Fourth Earl of Orford.

Serendip was the Arab name for Ceylon (Sri Lanka since 1972), an island and independent state in the Indian Ocean south of India. The island is actually connected by Adam's Bridge to the Indian mainland. Ceylon was derived from Silan, the Hindi name for the island. Sri Lanka, on the other hand, is derived from *Sri,* a respectful title of address prefixed to a man's name in India, and *Lanka,* the Sinhalese (an Indic language that is used by the majority of Lankans) word for the island.

shanghai

Shanghai is a commercial city (population 10,820,000) and a treaty port near the mouth of the Chiang Jiang River in eastern China. It was attacked and occupied by the Japanese in 1932 and by the Communists in 1949. Since the Communists finally opened China to tourism, a great many people have applied for visas and traveled there. However, travel to China was not always popular, particularly for sailors. In the nineteenth century, in fact, shipowners had a difficult time securing able-bodied seamen for such voyages because of the dangers of ocean travel in those days, and the long separation from loved ones. Accordingly, shipowners directed their agents to recruit U.S. seamen by any means, including abduction, alcohol, drugs, deceit, or a combination of all of the above.

Shanghai finally went verbal (it was transformed from a noun to a verb) and developed the sense of obtaining a crew by force or trickery. *Shanghai* has more recently been generalized to mean to compel unwilling people to do anything at all.

Shangri-la

Fiction is credited with introducing many a new word into the English language, including **Lilliputian** and **Utopia.** *Shangri-la,* another example of this kind of literary word coinage, is defined as an imaginary paradise on earth, especially a remote and exotic place.

Shangri-la was coined by James Hilton (1900–1954) in a best-selling book entitled *Lost Horizon* (1933). Hilton's *Shangri-la* was an imaginary place in the Himalayan mountains where a group of fictional travelers became stranded. They soon discovered that no one who lived in that magical place ever grew old. Hilton, a Cambridge University graduate, was born in Leigh, Lancashire, England. In addition to *Lost Horizon,* he wrote *Goodbye Mr. Chips,* another very popular best seller. Both books were made into movies which brought Hilton to the U.S. in the mid-thirties to work on the movie versions of his books.

The author's allusion to a mythical place where nobody grows old struck a popular chord with his readers. The quest for the Fountain of Youth is ageless and explains why people spend thousands of dollars on health **spas,** diets, and plastic surgery to reverse or retard the aging process. About all we can really do is slow down the inevitable and improve the quality of life so that our retirement home will be more like a *Shangri-la* than a **Hades.**

sherry/port

There are a great number of fortified wines, those in which spirits, usually brandy, are added to increase their strength or alcoholic content. Fortified wines have 18 to 21 percent alcohol content, as opposed to regular wines that have an alcoholic content of 8 to 14 percent. The stronger wines include such widely known and savored toponymous wines as Marsala from Sicily, Malaga from Spain, Tokay from Hungary, Madeira from the Island of Madeira, and, of course, *port* from Porto in Portugal, as well as *sherry* from Jerez de la Frontera, Spain. The wide popularity of *port* and *sherry* is confirmed by the fact that both are lower-cased unlike most other fortified wines.

Porto is a district of northwest Portugal where *port* is simply an anglicized version of Porto. *Sherry,* on the other hand, is a case (which is a good way to buy it) in which a man's name was transubstantiated into wine—etymologically speaking, of course. The word *sherry,* you see, was derived from the name of an old Roman colony (itself named after Julius Caesar) called Caesaris, Caesar's City, in southwest Spain near Cadiz. Caesaris was later rendered to *Xeres* by the Spanish and finally *Jerez.* It was from here that *sherry* wine was first produced. Somewhere along the way the English, who imported *sherry* in large quantities, anglicized *Xeres* to *sherris* and later to *sherry.*

Siamese twins

Siamese twins is a term now applied to babies who are physically joined together at birth. The first such twins to come to the attention of the world were Chang and Eng (1811–1874) born in

Bangkok, Thailand (prior to 1939 it was known as Siam) to a Chinese father and half-Chinese mother. Chang and Eng were joined at the chest by a short, tubular cartilaginous band. The medical community agreed that separating the two would be fatal. These twins were discovered by an Englishman who immediately realized their commercial potential. They left Bangkok, Thailand, in 1829 and went on a worldwide exhibition tour which included the United States. After amassing $60,000, a substantial fortune in those days, they bought a farm in North Carolina and received the surname of Bunker by action of the North Carolina legislature.

Chang and Eng married two North Carolina sisters, Sarah and Adelaide Yates, and became naturalized citizens. Chang had ten children while Eng had nine, all normal. On January 16, 1874, in their home in Mt. Airy, North Carolina, Eng awakened to find Chang dead. Eng died three hours later. Chang and Eng were successful farmers and considered trustworthy by their neighbors. Their wives, however, were so quarrelsome that it was necessary to separate them. Thereafter they maintained two households at which the twins alternately resided.

Siberia

In 1830 Andrew Jackson (1767–1845), the seventh president of the United States (1829–1837), ordered "all Indian tribes be removed to the West of the Mississippi . . . to the Siberia of the West." This was the first appearance in print, according to the *Oxford English Dictionary*, of the use of *Siberia* in a general sense to mean any undesirable or isolated locale, or job, to which one is assigned for punishment, a mark of disfavor, or the like. Siberia is a region of the Soviet Union in North Asia from the Ural Mountains to the Pacific. The word *Siberia* is probably derived from the Mongolian word *shibir* meaning marsh.

During the Communist rule in Russia, which began in 1917, Siberia developed a reputation as a place of punishment to which dissidents were sent to work in the labor camps and salt mines of that cold and barren region. The Communists, however, were not the first of the Russian rulers to use Siberia as a means of punishment. For centuries, the Czars had been using Siberia for penal purposes. Catherine the Great (1729–1796), for instance, banished General Grigori Potemkin (see **Potemkin village**) to that frozen wasteland for his perfidy in the Crimea. And if that was not punishment enough, the Czars *rubbed salt* (probably from the infamous Siberian salt mines) in the wounds of those unfortunate people who had incurred their disfavor by making them work in those very same mines.

slave

War has been responsible for countless new words and strange new uses for many old ones. The word *slave* is an example of the drastic downgrading of a once glorious word. The change in the English usage of this servile word was brought about by the repeated subjugation of a people, the Slavonians, by western conquerors.

During the Middle Ages, the eastward invasions of the Germans and Venetians caused whole populations of *Slavic* people to be enslaved. Slavonia is presently a region of Yugoslavia. In the Slavic language, the word *slav* meant glory, which is an indication of how these very proud and fierce warriors thought about themselves.

After their subjugation, however, *slav* came to be synonymous with servitude, and finally entered the English language as *slave,* a person who is the property of another. Incidentally, the universal word for hello or goodbye, *ciao,* comes from the Italian *shiavo,* meaning, "I am your slave." Ciao!

sleazy

When a manufacturer allows the quality of his or her product to slide, or fails to prevent cheap copies of it from entering the marketplace, the results can be disastrous. *Sleazy*, defined as contemptibly low, or mean, is a case in point. I shall examine the *fabric* of this product and word that went bad.

Sleazy is an alteration of Silesia, a region of Eastern Europe that was assigned to Poland as a result of the Potsdam Conference in 1945. It was from this area that a fine cloth lining was woven and exported. But, as is so often the case, cheap knock-offs (imitations) quickly flooded the market, and the quality of the fabric, as well as the word, rapidly deteriorated.

In 1967 a variation of *sleazy*, *sleaze*, meaning a contemptibly low or vulgar person, appeared. The fruit of this word loom also includes these recent variations on the theme: *sleazo*, or *sleazoid*, something sleazy or pornographic; *sleazeball* or *sleazebag*, a sleazy person; *sleazemonger*, a producer or seller of nasty entertainment; and *sleazebucket*, nasty. And there you have the *sleaze factor*, which, by the way, is a term used to describe the corrupt elements of a political administration.

sodomy. See **sybarite**.

Soho/SoHo

This tale of two cities features nicknames of districts within two of the world's greatest cities, New York and London, each having separate origins and character. The oldest of these neighborhoods, *Soho*, in the West End of London, has enjoyed a rejuvenation from the days when it was notable for its ethnic diversity, restaurants, night clubs, prostitution, sex movies, and other **sleazy** entertainment. All of this changed in the 1980s as rents climbed and it became more establishment-oriented, but still known for its restaurants. *Soho*, once the preserve of people hunting for entertainment, was originally derived from *soho*, a hunting cry (like "yoicks") which described the object of the hunt, in this case usually a hare.

SoHo, like **Tribeca** is an acronym that describes a delightful district of New York City. (So)uth of (Ho)uston (pronounced Howstin), north of Canal Street, west of Lafayette, and east of Sixth Avenue. This charming area has emerged since 1960 out of a part of the city noted primarily for small warehouses. Today, it is distinguished by its many art galleries, studios, restaurants, and shops.

solecism

Current linguistic theory holds that most of the European languages, as well as those of Iran, the Indian subcontinent, and parts of Asia, were descended from a single language, Indo-European, and are therefore all placed within the Indo-European family of languages. As the tribes of this first language group emigrated and were isolated for a time, their languages began to differ, at first slightly, and later quite markedly.

The ancient Greeks were known to be great colonizers, having established colonies throughout the Mediterranean area including Naples, an Italian city originally called *Neopolis,* new city; and Sybaris, another Italian city from which comes the English word **sybarite.** The Greeks also established a colony at Soloi in Cilicia (southeastern Asia Minor, now Turkey). As the years went by, differences in pronunciation of Greek words by Soloi citizens became noticeable. The Greeks called this nonstandard dialect spoken by the Cilicians, *soloikismos,* a word that survives today as *solecism* and means a nonstandard use of grammatical construction, a violation of etiquette, or even a mistake.

The impact of separation from the main branch of a language can be observed in the American and Australian dialects. I suspect that the English think of these differences as quaint little *solecisms.*

spa

In the town where I grew up, New Rochelle, New York, there was an ice cream parlor named the Boston Spa. It was a favorite spot for young and old. The word *spa,* in addition to being a soda fountain, is also defined as a mineral spring or a resort place having such a spring. The word *spa* came from the name of a famous resort town in Belgium, Spa, which was well known for its medicinal mineral springs. After the turn of the century, the popularity of mineral spring resorts declined, but today, they are becoming popular once again. *Spa,* however, has retained its healthful sense with its current generic use as a term for today's exercise facility—*the health spa.*

The use of *spa* for a soda fountain is out of vogue nowadays, but because of the interest in physical fitness, *spa* has been usurped by these new temples dedicated to the body beautiful.

Spain, castles in

For some people, writing a book may seem little more than an attempt to build a *castle in Spain.* This idiom was probably borrowed from the French whose equivalent is *chateaux en Espagne,* as well as *chateaux en Aise,* castles in the air. Both expressions mean a fanciful or impractical notion or hope; a daydream.

This venerable colloquialism was contained in a book that is part of the English incunabula (books printed before 1501 during the first stage of movable type). The book, entitled *Jason,* was published by William Caxton in 1475, and contained the idiom in the following sentence: "He began to make castellis in Spaygne as lovers doo." Caxton's press, the first one in England, rapidly increased the spread of English literature, and was responsible for stabilizing the form of English (the London dialect), which is spoken by seven hundred million people throughout the world today.

The best theory for the selection of Spain as the sight of these imaginary castles purports that it resulted from the Moorish domination of Spain that commenced in the eleventh century and lasted several hundred years. During the Moorish control of Spain, the environment was inhospitable to Christian interlopers, especially those wishing to build castles there.

spaniel, cocker

The intense rivalry between European states during the Middle Ages resulted in some interesting international ethnic slurs. For instance, years ago the Englishmen's hatred for their Iberian rivals drove them to convert the word *Spaniard,* a Spanish person, to *espaynel,* meaning a Spanish dog. So common was this derogatory epithet that it is used to this day, though rarely, in its modern form, *spaniel,* a word that is also defined as a fawning, cringing person.

Spaniel was also used to describe a pleasing sweet-dispositioned dog, the *cocker,* that was bred and trained to flush small birds, especially woodcocks. The dog eventually became known as the *cocker spaniel,* or literally the Spanish dog that flushes woodcocks.

Today, the *cocker spaniel* is one of the most popular dogs in the United States. They are used primarily as pets and show dogs, and rarely for hunting.

Spanish fly

As part of the unofficial initiation into the world of adult sexuality, most young men are exposed to an overload of fact and myth relating to the sexual arousal of the opposite sex. While I have no personal experience with the effects of *Spanish fly,* I have uncovered some interesting information on its origin, which I hope will arouse your interest. *Spanish fly,* for the uninitiated, is a preparation of powdered blister beetle, especially the *Spanish fly*, used medicinally as a diuretic, and more commonly as an aphrodisiac.

The first thing to learn about the three-quarter-inch long *Spanish fly* is that it is not a fly at all, but actually belongs to the blister beetle family, *Meloidae*. These are found in abundance in Spain, which explains their name. A substance called cantharidin can be extracted from this beetle's wing cases, which in its raw state is capable of blistering the skin. Well, I might not know much about the amorous effects of *Spanish fly*, but I do have personal experience with two old-fashioned stimulants: a dozen roses or a box of chocolate candy. Both have beneficial effects and I can recommend them highly.

Spartan. See **laconic.**

spruce tree/spruce beer/ spruce (up)/Prussian blue

You may be wondering how *Prussian blue* got mixed in with the *spruces* in the title of this segment. Well, while they might not appear to be related, they most definitely are. The connection between these words is interesting, but first let me tell you about Prussia, the place that inspired them. Prussia was carved out by the Hohenzollern family who came to power in 1415. At its peak in the late 1800s, Prussia, extending from Belgium and the Netherlands in the west to Russia in the east, included two-thirds of Germany and all of the Baltic states. It also was bounded in the north by the North and Baltic Seas and in the south by Austria and Hungary.

In the Middle Ages, Prussia was known to the English as Pruceland. The Pruce tree was a coniferous evergreen that was native to Pruce, and beer made from the extracts of the Pruce tree was called Pruce beer. Actually, *Pruce* or *Prussia* is a contraction of *Borussi,* the Baltic name for the inhabitants of East Prussia. Around the fourteenth century, Pruce gained an "S" and became *Sprucia.* In the sixteenth century, it was very popular to imitate the fashions of the noblemen of Sprucia, and someone so attired was said to be *Spruce* and later *spruce,* meaning trim in dress or appearance; neat, smart, and dapper. Eventually, *Spruce* lost its "S" (I lost mine in real estate) and became *Prussia,* but *spruce beer, spruce (up),* and the *spruce tree* remain as relics of the earlier English name for Prussia.

Prussian blue is an English version of the French phrase, *bleu de Prusse,* a moderate to deep greenish-blue, first produced in Prussia.

stogie (stogy)/Conestoga wagons/stogas

During the great westward expansion that began in colonial times, a small town named Conestoga in Lancaster County, Pennsylvania, became a jumping-off place for those brave pioneers seeking land and freedom in the American West. It was in this town that a large covered wagon, named after the town, was manufactured. This horse-drawn vehicle, which was the moving van of its day, also was known as a prairie wagon. The *Conestoga wagons* provided a very bumpy ride over the rough dirt roads of that period, and it took a tough breed of people to venture out into the western wilderness in them.

I have found no evidence to indicate that cigars were also manufactured in Conestoga, but I do know that a *stogie* (*stogy*) was a popular nickname for a long, thin, cheap cigar that was preferred by the very tough *Conestoga wagon* drivers. The word *stogie,* of course, came from the *-stoga* in *Conestoga.* These drivers also wore a special boot called *stogas,* once again named after this famous town.

Stoic/stoic/stoical/stoicism

The great thinkers of the ancient Greek civilization were often associated with a special place where their disciples would gather to be indoctrinated by them. The building, park, or section of the town where a particular philosopher would hold forth frequently became linked with him. Through the millennia, such placenames eventually developed a distinct but related meaning—for example, **academy, lyceum,** and **stoic.**

The *Stoic* school of philosophy was founded by Zeno about 300 B.C. Zeno was born in Citium on the island of Cypress. He was originally a merchant, but later went to Athens and became a thinker and teacher. Zeno held that "the supreme duty of a wise man is the complete and supreme submission to divine will." Additionally, Zeno felt that, "People should be free from passion and unmoved by grief and joy." Currently, a person can be referred to as *stoical* (or *stoic*) regardless of whether he or she knows anything about Zeno or not, for such a person is defined as one who is calm or passive by nature.

The *Stoa Poikile,* the painted porch, was a roofed porch supported by columns. It was here that Zeno taught. The porch featured fresco paintings depicting scenes from the Trojan War.

stygian

The Styx is a river that **meanders** through Greek mythology. It is across this underworld river that the dead were ferried on their way to **Hades.** The English word *stygian* is derived from Greek and has come to mean gloomy and dark, infernal, or hellish. The Styx also played a prominent role in the defeat of Achilles, according to legend.

It was in this river that the baby Achilles was dipped by his mother, Thetis, to make him invulnerable to his enemies. During one of the battles of the Trojan War, Achilles was shot with an arrow in the heel. This became the only part of his body that was vulnerable, because his heels had been cupped by his mother during his Styx dunking and had never gotten wet; they were therefore left unprotected. Achilles' accomplishments and death were immortalized in Homer's *Iliad*.

The ancient Greek mythological religion apparently held that the climate of the Styx and nearby Hades was forbiddingly cold. For, you see, the word *Styx* initially was fashioned from an earlier Greek word that meant cold, or frost. By contrast, later Christian theologians found that hell was hotter than, well, Hades.

suede

The Swedes have provided a soft touch for the French (and the rest of us) who called the velvety soft gloves manufactured there *gants de Suede,* which translates into English as Swedish gloves or gloves of Sweden. The Swedish people created gloves (1855–1860) made from the very finest napped leather, which they exported to France and elsewhere. *Suede* is made by holding the skin against a buffing wheel. The rough surface of the wheel is made so by treating it with emery or carborundum abrasives. In this way, a soft supple nap is raised on the leather. The word *suede,* therefore, does not denote leather of a specific animal, but all leathers or cloths so treated. The best *suede* leather comes from smaller animals such as sheep and pigs.

One cloth material made to look and feel like *suede* is UltraSuede (a trademarked product). Since the time our ancestors lived in caves, people have always enjoyed the feel of leather next to their skin, especially soft *suede*. UltraSuede™, however, is far easier to maintain and is, accordingly, very popular. *Ultra,* by the way, is a Latin word meaning beyond. So UltraSuede actually translates as beyond Sweden. In fact, UltraSuede, a nonwoven synthetic fabric, was invented in 1971 by a U.S. firm,

Spring Mills, Inc., of Spring Mills, South Carolina, which you must agree, is quite a bit beyond Sweden.

sybarite/sodomy

Shakespeare, in *Julius Caesar* (1599–1600) wrote that, "The evil men do lives after them; The good is often interred with their bones." This is certainly true of the people of Sybaris, an ancient Greek colony in southern Italy founded in 720 B.C. The inhabitants of this ancient *tinseltown* were famous for their wealth and luxurious way of living. Their legendary life style was the origin of our English word *sybarite,* meaning one who is given to wanton luxury and sensual pleasures. Life in the fast lane softened the Sybarites and eventually led to their defeat by the Crotoniates in 510 B.C., but their name lingers on, albeit in a derogatory way. Similar dubious immortality was achieved by the residents of Sodom and Gomorrah, cities in the plain of Jordan (ancient Palestine), also notorious for wickedness. The legacy of the Sodomites is the word *sodomy,* meaning deviate sexual practices.

TTTTTTTTTTTTT T TTTTTTTTTTTTT

tarantella

Ancient cures took many strange forms including a lively dance, which, at the time, was considered to be a sure cure for the bite of a tarantula. This large hairy spider was capable of inflicting a very painful but not fatal bite. The dance was called the *tarantella,* a lively whirling dance that was thought to be a cure for tarantism—the effect of the tarantula's bite on humans.

The King Kong of the spider kingdom, the tarantula, was plentiful in Taranto, Italy, which was founded by the Greeks in 700 B.C. and which they called Taras. It appears that the town was originally named for its large tarantula population. It is assumed that the lively 6/8 time of the *tarantella* helped to more quickly dissipate the effect of the spider's bite on the body.

tariff

United States *tariff* reform was originated in the 1890s and free trade has more or less remained U.S. policy ever since. A *tariff* is a duty or tax levied against imports or exports. There are two schools of thought on the origin of *tariff,* and I shall try to reconcile both of these theories without *taxing* your mind too severely. The first of these hypotheses suggests that *tariff* is derived from an Arab word meaning mathematical casting of accounts.

Tariff is also traceable to Tarifa, a seaport 51 miles south of Cadiz, Spain, 20 miles from Gibraltar, and considered to be the southernmost point in Europe. This port, a one-time Roman settlement, was controlled by African pirates during the Moorish occupation of this part of Spain. These Mediterranean freebooters forced ships passing through the Straits of Gibraltar (see **Gibraltar**) to pay duties, a form of blackmail that came to be known as a *tariff.* This forced levy assured safe passage to and from the Mediterranean Sea.

The apparent contradiction in these two plausible explanations of *tariff's* origin is more understandable when one realizes how often the meanings of modern words are influenced by two or more origins or events. *Tariff* has also come to generally mean a bill, cost, or change.

tartar/catch a tartar/ tartare steak

In the thirteenth century, various tribes, chiefly Mongolian and Turkish, known as *Tatars* (also *Tartars*), originally under the leadership of Genghis Khan, overran Asia and much of Eastern Europe. The Tatar ASSR (Autonomous Soviet Socialist Republic) is in the eastern part of, and at the bend of, the Middle Volga. Through centuries of intermarriage, the Tartars have calmed down a bit but have left in their wake several idioms attesting to their fierce fighting spirit. *Tartar,* for instance, is a synonym for an ill-tempered person.

To catch a tartar is another idiom, much like to have a bear or tiger by the tail, meaning to deal with something that proves to be unexpectedly troublesome or powerful. *Tartare (tartar) steak* led to the development of the **hamburger.** It consists of ground beefsteak seasoned with salt and pepper and served uncooked, often mixed with a raw egg and garnished with capers and onions, among other things. I am not sure about the origin of *tartar sauce*, a **mayonnaise** dressing for fish and seafood with chopped pickles, olives, capers, and green herbs added, but it too was probably inspired by these same Tartars.

Thames on fire, never set the

The Thames (pronounced tems) is a river that flows eastward for 209 miles directly through the heart of London, England, on its way to the North Sea. There are several proposed origins for the word *Thames,* but I have settled on the Celtic version, which concludes that it originally meant smooth water. There are also several versions of this featured phrase which has come to mean he or she will never do something remarkable. I have decided to stay in the *mainstream* on this phrase and pray that my explanation will not inflame anyone.

I must credit the *Dictionary of Word Origins* by Joseph T. Shipley for the most plausible of these etymologies. Shipley suggests that the Thames in this curious phrase is based on the early English word *temse,* a wooden tube in which the piston of the old spinning wheel ran up and down. If one worked very fast the *temse* might begin to smoke. The *temse,* according to Shipley, was later mistakenly confused with, and spelled like, the river Thames.

It is interesting to note that the Germans substituted the Rhine for the Thames in this phrase, while the French inserted the Seine instead. I must assume that the continental versions of this popular English phrase resulted from the assumption that the placename in this idiom was the great English river, and people mistakenly substituted their own local rivers for the original Thames.

Tiananmen.

See **Chinese solution.**

Timbuktu. See **Dan to Beersheba.**

tobacco

Although the etymology of *tobacco* is somewhat cloudy, I shall endeavor to clear the smoke surrounding it. One thing is certain—reading about *tobacco* is not injurious to your health.

In 1498, Christopher Columbus discovered Tobago, an island in the West Indies, currently part of Trinidad and Tobago. Columbus saw the Indians of Tobago exhaling smoke through their nostrils. They used a Y-shaped pipe which they called a *tabaco*. In the Taino language of the Caribbean, *tabaco* was a roll of *tobacco* leaves similar to a small, present-day cigar. According to Eric Partridge, both words were probably influenced by the island of Tobago. The first *tobacco* to reach Europe was from the West Indies and South America.

It is believed that in 1613, John Rolfe, the husband of the famous Indian princess, Pocahontas, was the first member of an English colony (Jamestown) to export *tobacco* to England. Rolfe's *tobacco* seed, it is thought, was of the Orinoco variety grown in the West Indies and in South America.

It took courage on the part of these colonial farmers to cultivate the *tobacco* crop and hope that it would *catch fire* in England, but it did. So *put that in your pipe and smoke it,* which is exactly what the Englishmen did.

Toledo, Holy

The holy city of Toledo is nestled in the central region of Spain. Toledo tolerated strong secular and religious interests. On the one hand, Toledo was and is renowned for the superb quality of its sword blades and its beautifully hammered metalwork that decorates gifts and jewelry manufactured there. But Toledo was and is also famous for its handsome mosques and cathedrals. Apparently the word was not mightier than the sword in Toledo because the two industries (religion and swordmaking) existed side by side for many centuries.

It was the religious nature of Toledo that gave rise to the expression, *Holy Toledo,* which is heard occasionally today as an expression of surprise, awe, and mild vexation. The popularity of *Holy Toledo* was heightened by what is called reduplication in grammatical parlance. Reduplication is simply the repetition of a grammatical pattern, which in this case is produced by preceding the first four-letter sound, Toly, in Toledo with Holy. Well, enough of this reduplicative *razzle dazzle.* (Oops, there's another one!)

Thule, ultima.

See **Dan to Beersheba.**

Tribeca

New York City is noted for its ethnic and avant-garde districts such as Yorkville, Greenwich Village, East Village, **SoHo,** and now *Tribeca,* a trendy new word for an old section of the city. *Tribeca* is an acronym formed from the words *Tri*angle *Be*low *Ca*nal. It was coined in the mid-1970s, according to my New York Public Library source, by a creative but otherwise unknown New York Realtor as an ear-catching name for an area that he was trying to promote.

Tribeca is not a legal entity and, therefore, its geography varies depending on who is defining it. All agree that *Tribeca* is bounded on the north and west by Canal Street and West Street, respectively. But the eastern boundary is variously set as Courtlandt Alley, Church Street, and West Broadway. For its southern boundary you can choose between Chambers and Barclay Streets.

Tribeca is slightly north of the World Trade Center and Battery Park City and is worth a trip through it on your next visit to **The Big Apple.**

Trojan Horse

Here is a horse, not only of a different color, but of a different composition as well—a *Trojan Horse.* The story that was recounted in Homer's *Iliad,* written between 800 and 700 B.C., told of an event that determined the outcome of the Trojan War in 1200 B.C. between the Greeks and Trojans.

Idiomatically, a *Trojan Horse* is a person or thing intended to undermine or destroy from within. The outcome of the Trojan War was decided by a Greek deception. According to Homer, the Greeks left a huge hollow wooden horse outside the gates of Troy. Assuming that the horse was a peace offering, the Trojans brought it within the city walls. The Trojans, however, did not know that the horse concealed Greek soldiers inside. That night the Greek soldiers crept out of the horse's belly and opened the city gates for their fellow Greek soldiers who promptly conquered Troy.

This story also gave rise to the proverb, *beware of Greeks bearing gifts,* which has become generalized to mean be wary of gifts offered from unlikely sources—a truth the Trojans learned the hard way.

turkey/theatrical turkey/ talk turkey/cold turkey

The large bird that graces our holiday table also provides us with a feast of interesting idioms. It was, however, a simple case of mistaken identity that caused it to be called a *turkey* in the first place. Join my old-fashioned *turkey shoot* (shooting match) as I pluck out the truth of this big bird's origins.

In the Turkish language the word *turk* means strength, and *Turkey* is, therefore, the land of the strong people. The big bird that we call a *turkey* originated in Turkey and migrated to Europe through Asia.

The American *turkey*, the *meleagris gallopavo*, was mistaken by the early colonists for the guinea fowl of Turkey, which is an entirely different species. This error has never been corrected and so the bird continues to be popularly known as the *turkey*.

A *turkey* or theatrical flop got its name, according to an interesting theory, from a legitimate theater play that flopped very badly. The name of the show was *To Cage a Turkey*. After this *turkey*, all other *fowl* theatrical offerings were called *turkeys*.

To *talk turkey* came from the turkey course that graced many a holiday feast, and so to *talk turkey* means to get to the essential or central theme of a subject.

Cold turkey is a term used in selling to describe a cold call on a prospective client for which no appointment was made. The *cold turkey* idiom also describes the act of abruptly stopping one's dependence on cigarettes, alcohol, or drugs. In both cases, the expression describes the skin condition of the salesperson or drug addict who is going through a *cold turkey* experience; like a plucked *turkey* before it is placed in the oven, the skin is clammy white and covered with goose bumps (horripilation).

A person who is easily defrauded or deceived is also called a *turkey*. This usage comes from the fact that the *turkey* is considered to be easily deceived by hunters. There you have a pretty full plate of *turkey* and with all the trimmings too.

turquoise

Although *turquoise* can be found in many places—for example, Turkestan, Asia Minor, Persia, New Mexico, Colorado, Arizona, and Nevada—it was probably first exported to Europe from Turkey and thus the word *turquoise* came to mean the Turkish stone. *Turquoise* is an opaque, semiprecious stone that comes in various shades of blue and green. It consists primarily of hydrous phosphate of aluminum. Small quantities of iron give it a bluish color, while the presence of small amounts of copper imparts a greenish hue. The Egyptians prized this beautiful stone as early as 4000 B.C.

Fake *turquoise* is sometimes referred to as *odontolite,* which is nothing more than crushed bone colored blue with phosphate of iron. *Odontolite* is a clever word construction that combines two Greek elements that literally mean tooth stone.

tuxedo

The *tuxedo* was first worn by Griswold Lorillard (see **tobacco**) in 1886 at the Tuxedo Park resort club near Tuxedo Lake, New York, about 40 miles north of New York City. Lorillard, according to tradition, was tired of wearing the more formal and cumbersome full dress *tailcoat* and had his tailor cut the tails off. This abbreviated fashion quickly caught on and was named for the place where it first appeared. *Tuxedo,* by the way, is derived from the Lanape Indian word *p'tuksit* meaning a wolf. (I suspect that many a *p'tuksit* has worn a *tuxedo* over the years.) Tuxedo Lake was an exclusive high-rent neighborhood in the nineteenth century, and its list of residents included, along with Lorillard, such names as Gould, Astor, and Harriman.

In addition to *tuxedo,* there is a whole wardrobe of confusing terminology relating to the use of formal attire. The dictionary terms, however, proved imprecise. In order to sort this all out, I contacted my good friend John Allegro, a formalwear expert, who set me straight about the current definition of these terms.

Glossary of Formalwear Terms

tuxedo a dinner jacket of black or dark blue with satin lapels. The outfit usually includes black trousers often having satin stripes down the sides, a bow tie, and a cummerbund.

semiformal dress denotes dress that can range from a dark business suit to a *tuxedo*.

formal dress calls for a tailcoat or *tuxedo*.

black tie literally calls for a black bow tie with a *tuxedo*. Today, however, a tie and cummerbund of any color can be worn.

white tie requires the wearing of a white bow tie with tails (tailcoat). This attire is very popular at proms, special cotillions, and extremely formal affairs.

formalwear clothing, such as a tuxedo, designed or customarily worn on formal occasions; formal or semiformal attire for evenings.

cutaway a man's formal daytime coat (usually worn between 10:00 A.M. and 2:00 P.M.) with the front portion cut away from the waist and curving around to the tails in the back. This type of wear is used primarily for weddings. The outfit includes an Oxford gray coat with gray striped pants and pearl gray vest.

evening wear formal or semiformal attire for evening wear, also called evening clothes.

tailcoat (also tails, dress coat, swallow-tailed coat) a man's fitted coat (see *cutaway*), usually black and worn as part of full evening dress.

Tweed/tweeds/tweedy

The word *tweed,* describing a two-threaded fabric originally of Scotland, can be traced to a Scottish word that was either miswritten by a Scottish weaver or misread by a London merchant. The yarn that explains this mixup is attested to by the best authorities. Sometime in the early part of the nineteenth century, a weaver in Scotland near the River Tweed shipped his production of twill fabric to James Locke, a London merchant. The Scotch word for the two-threaded twill fabric, *tweel,* was misread as *Tweed* by persons receiving it in the London firm, who assumed that the yard goods were from the area of the River Tweed.

Tweed, therefore, is simply the result of mistaken identity. The true source of the word *twill* (tweel) is the *twi* element, meaning two, that is found in such words as *twilight* (second light), *between,* and *twain. Tweed* is currently defined as a coarse wool cloth, either hand spun and hand woven in Scotland or reproduced, often by machine, elsewhere. *Tweeds* are garments made of this cloth, while *tweedy* refers to persons wearing or favoring tweeds, especially as a mark of a casual, sporty, or intellectual way of life.

uuuuuuuuuu**U**uuuuuuuuuu

Ural-altaic. See **Altaic.**

utopia

Sir Thomas More (1478–1535), who was Lord Chancellor in the realm of England's King Henry VIII, was a statesman, philosopher, and author. Historians believe that he was describing the recently discovered Americas when he wrote a book entitled *Utopia* in 1516, because he knew it did not exist in the Europe of his day.

Sir Thomas' book *Utopia* describes an imaginary paradisical land where the institutions and policies are governed by reason alone. Reportedly, More relied heavily on the picture of the New World described by Amerigo Vespucci.

More, an Oxford scholar, apparently coined the word for this perfect paradise by combining the Greek elements *ou*, not; *topos*, a place; and *ia*, a region. Literally, therefore, *Utopia* was no place on earth.

V

valhalla

The ancient Scandinavians were notorious for their love of battle. Known by such names as the Danes, Vikings, and Norsemen, they were fearless warriors whose appearance struck terror in the hearts of the inhabitants of western and northern Europe. In fact, if it had not been for Alfred the Great, the English king who prevented the Danes from capturing all of Britain, I might be writing this in Danish instead of English.

It is easier to understand the Scandinavians' love of war when you learn about the mythical rewards that awaited those soldiers who died bravely or heroically in battle. They believed that such men would go to *Valhalla,* the great hall of their god Odin. There they would go out each morning to do battle, only to return to the massive hall of *valhalla* at noon to receive a sumptuous meal served by the beautiful blond Valkyries (battle maidens). The walls of *Valhalla* were said to be made of gold while the roof was made of battle shields. *Valhalla* literally means hall of the slain. It is no wonder that these fearless soldiers were so eager to fight. *Valhalla* must have seemed like a very attractive reward for giving one's life honorably in battle. (Were it not so overused a pun, you might say that they were *dying* to get there.) *Valhalla* has also come to mean a place or sphere assigned to persons worthy of special honors.

Vandal

One can easily imagine the Vandals of ancient Vandalia turning in their graves and thinking, "Okay, so we got a little carried away when we sacked Rome in A.D. 455, but can't you just let bygones be bygones? Surely it isn't fair to blame us for every incident involving damage to property that has occurred since the Rome thing." For a long time since that memorable trashing of Rome, the Vandals have been immortalized by the toponymous word, *vandal*, which describes a person who willfully or ignorantly destroys something beautiful or valuable.

The Vandals were a Germanic tribe that originally lived along the southern coasts of what are now Norway, Sweden, and Denmark before they migrated in 100 B.C. to a region below the Baltic Sea and settled in Silesia (see **sleazy**) and Galicia (see **galoshes**). They later moved into Spain and Gaul. Things really got into high gear for the Vandals under King Genseric who ruled this unruly group from 428–477, during which time the Vandals conquered North Africa. In addition, it was under Genseric's command that the "rumble in Rome" occurred.

The attack on Rome not only started Rome on its descent, but also created a bad press for the Vandals. Their name, however, did not become synonymous with destruction until 1793 when a French priest, Henri Gregoire, used the word *vandalisme* to describe the destruction of works of art by French Revolutionary fanatics. *Vandalisme* has since been borrowed by the English who anglicized it to *vandalism*. The Vandals could not have been all bad because their name has also been immortalized in the names of three U.S. cities named Vandalia in the states of Ohio, Illinois, and Mississippi.

vaudeville

The region of Normandy, France, that produced William the Conqueror (1027–1087) was also the source of the word *vaudeville.* Webster defines *vaudeville* as "a stage show consisting of mixed specialty acts, including songs, dances, comic skits, acrobatic performances, etc." While *vaudeville* is now rare in the United States, fond memories remain.

Vaudeville is derived from Chanson du Vau de Vire, which is translated from the French as *Chanson,* song; *du,* of the; *Vau,* valley; *de,* of; *Vir,* a district in Calvados (Normandy), France.

This type of popular song called *vaudevire* and, later, *vaudeville* by the local townspeople, is believed to have been developed by Oliver Besselin, an entertainer of that region.

venetian (also venetion) blind/venetian blue/venetian red/ Venetian school/venetian glass

Venice, a beautiful city of northeastern Italy that consists of 118 islands situated on the Adriatic Sea, was founded in the fifth century A.D. by refugees from barbarian invasions. It is noted for its beautiful architecture, glass, and canals that provide the primary means of transportation in this truly unique city. Venice is also noted for the creation of the world's first **ghetto** to which the Jewish citizens of that city were banished in the early sixteenth century.

Here is a gondola full of Venetian toponyms:

venetian blind a window treatment having overlapping horizontal slats that may be opened or closed, especially one in which the slats may be raised and drawn together above the window by pulling a cord. These blinds were designed to provide privacy as well as to regulate the amount of light permitted into a room. *Venetian blinds* first became popular in the sixteenth century when they were called *persiani* by the Venetians who had earlier imported them from Persia. Some people believe that the window blind was originally developed by the Japanese, who made something similar out of bamboo rods.

venetian blue a strong blue to greenish-blue produced by the glass industry of that city.

venetian red a deep, strong reddish-brown.

Venetian school a group of artists including Battista, Tiepolo, and Canaletto, among others, all of whom came from and painted in Venice.

venetian glass ornamental glassware of the type made on the Venetian island of Murano and developed by Beroverio, a glassmaker who perfected a kind of transparent glass in 1463.

There are a number of other cities which are compared to Venice, among them are Brugge, "the Venice of Belgium," and Leningrad, "the Venice of the North (or Russia)."

verdigris

If someone should sidle up to you in a foreign country and say, "Pssst! Do you want to buy a genuine relic?" and shows you a small greenish or bluish metal figure, be careful, because it is undoubtedly a fake, although perhaps a very good one. The art of faking artifacts is very sophisticated. Any item made of copper, brass, or bronze, for example, can be given a bluish or green patina by applying acetic acid to it. This forms a copper sulphate, which without the aid of chemicals normally takes many years to form.

The bluish-greenish coating on such metals is called *verdigris,* a word that has, itself, aged rather nicely. It is derived from a much older phrase formed in several European languages, *vert de Grece,* which simply means green of Greece. There was apparently a good market for Greek antiques in Europe from Medieval days right up to modern times. Many of those items had a greenish patina on them.

Incidentally, *patina* is a film of incrustation, usually green, produced by surface oxidation. *Patina* comes from the English word *paten,* meaning a shallow dish, which at one time was undoubtedly made of copper, brass, or bronze, and in time became greenish. *Verdigris* is used commercially in dyeing, **calico,** printing, and green paint. It is also used in making salves and liniments. *Verdigris* (copper sulphate) is poisonous. (My uncle discovered this the hard way when he swallowed some and became a relic himself. But, oh what a marvellous finish!)

Vichy (vichy) water/vichyssoise

France has been a virtual spring of word origins having to do with water, such as **artesian wells;** Perrier, a sparkling water produced in France that has become almost a generic word for all such waters; and, of course, *vichy water. Vichy water* flows from a natural spring in Vichy, a city in central France, the provisional capital of unoccupied France from 1940 to 1942 (The Vichy Government). This special water, used as a treatment for digestive disturbances and gout, contains sodium bicarbonate, along with other alkaline salts and minerals. *Vichy water,* now replaced by various seltzer-type digestive aids, became synonymous with all natural and artificial aids of this type.

Vichyssoise (pronounced vish ē swăz) is a delicious cream

soup of potatoes and leek usually served chilled and often garnished with chopped chives. It is a special recipe of Vichy, France.

Vietnamization. See **balkanization.**

Wall Street

Although *Wall Street* is only seven blocks long, it has become an international nickname for the U.S. financial district. Peter Stuyvesant, governor of the Dutch settlement of New Amsterdam, was indirectly responsible for this toponymous sobriquet. In 1692 Stuyvesant ordered the construction of a high wooden barricade at the northern end of his tiny settlement to protect it from attacks by the English and local Indian tribes. In 1699 the wall was removed and both sides of the street quickly built up. And although the wall came tumbling down, the name for this street, *Wall,* remained.

According to *Listening to America* by Stuart Berg Flexner, on May 17, 1792, a century after the wall was built, a group of 24 merchants formed the first U.S. stock exchange. This historic event occurred under an old buttonwood tree on *Wall Street* where they met to buy and sell securities. Later, this alliance became the New York Stock Exchange, which built its headquarters on *Wall Street* in 1863.

One does not have to have a *Wall Street* business address to be a *Wall Streeter,* because this latter term is reserved for a person employed by institutions in the financial district.

waterloo

At La Belle Alliance, three miles southeast of Waterloo, Belgium, Napoleon Bonaparte was defeated in 1815 by the British under Wellington and the Prussians under Blucher. It was Napoleon's final defeat and it finished him politically. As a result of the crushing nature of this defeat at that place, *waterloo* has become generalized to mean a disastrous defeat of any nature.

As a postscript to this etymology, it is interesting to note that the names of the three principal players in this battle—Wellington, Blucher, and Napoleon—have become immortalized with eponyms (words that come from people's names). The *Wellington boot* extends to the top of the knee in front but is cut low in the back. *Beef Wellington* is a steak fillet with paté spread over it, then covered with pastry, and baked. A *napoleon* is a rectangular piece of pastry made with crisp, flaky layers filled with custard cream. Blucher, like Wellington, had a type of footwear that was developed for and named after him; the *blucher* is a high shoe or half boot, with the vamp and tongue usually made of one piece.

weiner. See **frankfurter.**

welsh

The origin of the toponymous verb *to welsh* differs greatly depending on which side of the Welsh Marches you live. I shall explain the origins of the Welsh name for these Celtic people, as well as the various origins of the idiom *to welsh* (welch) meaning failing to pay a debt.

The name *Wales* was bestowed upon a peninsula on the western coast of Great Britain by the Saxons who invaded Britain starting in A.D. 450. They called the Celtic residents of that place the Wealas, which meant a stranger or foreigner, not of Saxon origin. It was the Celts and Britons who escaped the invading Germanic tribes by fleeing to the Cambrian Mountains of Wales where they maintained their independence for hundreds of years.

There are several explanations for the idiom *to welsh*. Ernest Weekley suggests that it comes from the English nursery rhyme: "Taffy was a Welshman, Taffy was a thief, Taffy came to my house and stole a leg of beef."

The English version of this verb's origin proposes that Welsh racing bookies were known to take bets at English tracks only to disappear back to Wales without paying-off winning bettors. The Welsh explanation, according to Rosie Boycott, attributes this expression to an English bookie from Epson named Bob Welch, who stole the bets entrusted to him.

Welsh rabbit/rarebit

There are a great many instances in which euphemistic or humorous names were given to certain food preparations apparently to obscure their true identities or, perhaps, to improve their acceptance by the public. *Cape Cod turkey*, which is nothing more than cod fish, is a good example of this kind of food naming, as is *Coney Island gold*, a fancy name for mustard, applied to a **hot dog** (Coney Island). *Welsh rabbit*, a dish of melted cheese, usually mixed with ale or beer, milk, and spices served over toast, is another example of mock food names originally enjoyed by Welsh peasants.

Welsh rabbit, later known as *Welsh rarebit*, had nothing to do with Peter Cottontail. It was actually a poor substitute for a rabbit dish reserved for the aristocracy in Wales, Great Britain, in the late Middle Ages. *Rarebit* is nothing more than a jocular corruption of *rabbit* and first appeared in print in 1715–1725.

worsted/linsey-woolsey

I am about to spin a yarn (tell a story) or two about several woolen toponyms and idioms. And even though not all of these are toponyms, I think you will agree that they make interesting reading. The first of these, *worsted,* is a firm, textured, compactly twisted woolen yarn made from long-staple fibers. The word *worsted* was fashioned after the Medieval village of Worthstede, Norfolk, England. This village, now called Worthstead, was originally settled in the twelfth century by Flemish weavers who manufactured a special wool fabric there, now known as *worsted.* Here is a list of other wooly idioms.

A Glossary of Wooly Idioms

linsey-woolsey is a coarse linen wool fabric made at Lindsey in Suffolk, England. Colloquially, *linsey-woolsey* is any mixture that is incongruous or of poor quality; a jumble.

whole cloth was, originally, cloth made from the full width (broadcloth) of the loom. At one time in England, *whole cloth* meant good or solid, but its meaning has deteriorated because of unscrupulous merchants who began selling *whole cloth* that was pieced together, stretched, adulterated (with shoddy, see below) or not made on a full loom. *Whole cloth,* as a result, came to mean fictitious or without foundation.

shoddy is the fluff produced from the weaving process. Often the *shoddy* residue was mixed in with raw wool, reducing the quality of the yarn produced by such a mixture. *Shoddy,* which is derived from an older word, *shode,* meaning to shed, has come to mean of poor quality or inferior workmanship.

all wool and no shoddy has come to mean 100 percent quality with no reclaimed wool.

all wool and a yard wide means of high quality, genuine, reliable, in the best condition. This expression was first used by traveling cloth merchants who would convey the quality and full measurement of their cloth with this colloquialism.

woolgathering means absent-minded or indulging in daydreams. Back in the sixteenth century, servants and shepherds would wander about the fields in an aimless fashion picking up bits of fluff deposited by the sheep on fences, trees, and the like. The aimless manner in which they appeared to roam about the countryside gave rise to this expression.

pulling the wool over one's eyes is derived from the fact that at one time most men wore wool wigs. The idiom was derived from the practice of thieves who pulled the wool, or wig, down over a wig-wearer's eyes just before robbing him. This colloquialism has come to mean to deceive and is also responsible for the closely related term to *hoodwink*.

hoodwinking was the purse-snatcher's trick of pulling the wig down over a victim's eyes just before he grabbed his or her money. To *hoodwink* currently means to deceive or trick.

dyed in the wool has come to mean inveterate or confirmed. This idiomatic sense is derived from the fact that when wool cloth is dyed, the color may not be uniform throughout. If, however, the wool is dyed before it is spun, the cloths made from it will be consistent in color.

Xanadu

About 20 years ago, I was vacationing in the Bahamas near the Xanadu Hotel in Freeport. We were told that this exotic-sounding hotel was owned by none other than Howard Hughes who occupied the top floor. This Xanadu, I later discovered, turned out to be more of a prison for the reclusive industrialist than the paradise it was described as. A *Xanadu* is any place of great beauty or luxury, and is often used as a sort of elegant synonym for *paradise.*

Unlike **Shangri-la** and **Utopia,** *Xanadu* is not just another literary creation, but a real place. *Xanadu* first appeared in a 1797 poem entitled *Kubla Kahn* by the English poet Samuel T. Coleridge. Coleridge's source for *Xanadu* was Xandu, from an earlier book (1625) by Samuel Purchas entitled *Purchas, His Pilgrims.* Xandu was the name of a very beautiful palace where the great Kubla Kahn (1216–1294) "built; creating . . . a marvelous . . . palace of marble" in southeast Mongolia, according to the *Oxford English Dictionary*. The modern name for the site of Kahn's pleasure dome is the Chinese city of Shangtu.

YYYYYYYYYYYYY Y YYYYYYYYYYYYY

Young Turks

I was fascinated by a 1985 newspaper article about an unsuccessful attempt to overthrow the constitutional government of Thailand. The one aspect in the reporter's story that caught my attention was his use of the phrase *Young Turks* to describe the group that attempted the unsuccessful coup and, as a result, were probably executed for their trouble.

Since there seemed to be little likelihood of finding Turks in Thailand (despite the nice alliteration), I went directly to my library to uncover the answer to this enigma. I discovered that the idiom, *Young Turks,* stems from an earlier *coup d'etat* attempt by a group of young, restless Turkish revolutionaries. In 1908, during the waning days of the Ottoman Empire, these *Young Turks* banded together in an effort to restore parliamentary government in Turkey. Their attempt was successful.

Today, *Young Turk* is used to describe any group considered to be impatient with an existing regime, methods, and so on.

Bibliography

Barnett. *The Treasure of Our Tongue*. New York: Alfred A. Knopf, 1964.

Barnhart, Robert K. *The Barnhart Dictionary of Etymology*. New York: H.W. Wilson, 1988.

Boycott, Rosie. *Batty, Bloomers and Boycott*. New York: Peter Bedrich Books, 1983.

Brewer, E. Cobham. *Brewer's Dictionary of Phrase and Fable* (Centenary Edition, Revised). Ed. Ivor H. Evans. New York: Harper & Row, 1981 (original 1870).

Cassady, Frederic G. *Dictionary of American Regional English (DARE)*. Cambridge, Mass.: The Belknap Press of Harvard University Press, 1985.

Chapman, Robert L. *American Slang*. New York: Harper & Row, 1986.

Ciardi, John. *A Browser's Dictionary*. New York: Harper & Row, 1980.

Ciardi, John. *A Second Browser's Dictionary*. New York: Harper & Row, 1983.

Ciardi, John. *Good Words to You*. New York: Harper & Row, 1987.

Davies, Peter. *Success with Words*. Pleasantville, N.Y.: The Reader's Digest Association, 1983.

Eliot, T.S. *Old Possum's Book of Practical Cats*. New York: Harcourt, Brace & World, 1971.

Ewert, Neil. *Everyday Phrases*. Dorset, England: Blandford Press, 1986.

Farmer, J.S., and Henley, W.E. *A Dictionary of Slang*. Ware, England: Wordsworth Editions, 1987.

Flexner, Stuart Berg. *Listening to America*. New York: Simon & Schuster, 1982.

Freeman, Morton S. *The Story Behind the Word*. Philadelphia: ISI Press, 1985.

Bibliography

Funk, Charles. *Thereby Hangs a Tale*. New York: Harper & Row, 1985.

Funk, Wilfred. *Word Origins and Their Romantic Stories*. New York: Bell, 1978.

Giscard d'Estaing, Valerie-Anne. *The World Almanac of Inventions*. New York: World Almanac Publications, 1985.

Heller, Louis; Humeg, Alexander; and Dror, Malchah. *The Private Lives of English Words*. London: Routledge & Kegan Paul, 1985.

Hilliam, David. *Wordlore*. Scotland: W & R Chambers, 1984.

Holt, Alfred H. *Phrases and Word Origins*. New York: Dover, 1961 (original 1936).

Manchester, Richard B. *Amazing Facts: The Indispensable Collection of True Facts & Feats*. New York: Galahad Books, 1987.

McCrum, Robert; Cran, William; and MacNeil, Robert. *The Story of English*. New York: Viking Penguin, 1986.

Morris, William and Mary. *Morris Dictionary of Word and Phrase Origins*. New York: Harper & Row, 1971.

Morris, William and Mary. *Dictionary of Contemporary Usage* (Second Edition). New York: Harper & Row, 1985.

Nurnberg, Maxwell. *I Always Look Up the Word Egregious*. Englewood Cliffs, N.J.: Prentice Hall, 1981.

Partridge, Eric. *Origins; A Short Etymological Dictionary of Modern English*. New York: Greenwich House, 1983.

Radice, Betty. *Who's Who in the Ancient World*. Harmondsworth, England: Penguin, 1971.

Rawson, Hugh. *A Dictionary of Euphemisms and Other Doubletalk*. New York: Crown, 1981.

Rees, Nigel. *Why Do We Say . . . ?* Dorset, England: Blandford Press, 1987.

Room, Adrian. *A Dictionary of True Etymologies*. London: Routledge & Kegan Paul, 1986.

Safire, William. *Safire's Political Dictionary*. New York: Random House, 1978.

Sherk, William. *500 Years of New Words*. Garden City, N.Y.: Doubleday, 1983.

Shipley, Joseph T. *Dictionary of Word Origins*. New York: Philosophical Library, 1945.

Stimson, George. *A Book About a Thousand Things*. New York: Harper & Brothers, 1946.

Tuleja, Tad. *Curious Customs*. New York: Harmony Books, 1987.

Urdang, Lawrence. *Names and Nicknames of Places and Things*. New York: Meridien, 1987.

Walter, Don. *The Motown Story*. New York: Scribners, 1985.

Weekley, Ernest. *An Etymological Dictionary of Modern English.* New York: E.P. Dutton, 1921.

Wentworth, Harold, and Flexner, Stuart Berg. *Dictionary of American Slang*. New York: Thomas Y. Crowell, 1975.